SECRETS I STOLE FROM A PICKUP ARTIST

A STRAIGHT-UP, VERY REAL DATING GUIDE
FOR MEN

ZEPHANIAH NETZ

SOY SAUCE PUBLISHING

DISCLAIMER

This book is for adults only.

While this book is based on a true story, the names and descriptions of the characters have been changed to protect their identities. Any similarities in this book to actual persons, places, and/or events is purely coincidental. Any trademarks used in this text are properties of the respective trademark holders and have no relationship to the author or publisher of this book.

This book provides general advice for entertainment and education purposes only. The author and publisher disclaim any liability for any errors or omissions. The reader is responsible for their own actions and the author and publisher disclaim any liability for the actions of the reader. This book does not provide professional, medical, legal, or psychological advice of any kind. If the reader needs professional, medical, legal, or psychological advice of any kind, it is recommended that the reader seek a licensed professional in the field.

CONTENTS

INTRODUCTION

This book is like no other dating book you'll ever read in your life, I know they all say that, but what you have here in your hands is the ultimate book that contains all the magical secrets you'll ever need to unlock a woman's heart. And probably unbeknownst to you, a whole industry has been set up to hide these secrets from men, and who knows what they'll do to me for revealing them.

Yes, I stole these secrets from one of the best pickup artists in the business, and I promised I would never reveal them, and here I am writing a book spilling the beans, and you can call me an unhonorable, spineless, piece of dung for it, but it wasn't like that, like you don't even know the full story yet, so it would be a bit premature for you to judge me like that until you know all the itty bitty little details, doncha think? And anyway, why I wrote this book is a whole other matter we'll get into later.

For now, all you need to know is that what you're going to find in this book, are the real, uncut, ultimate, most legitimate secrets that exist on the planet, that those who are in the know can use to achieve massive success with women.

And my promise to you is that as long as you read

through all of the pages in this book and learn the secrets that I share and retain them in your memory, you can't not be successful with women. Actually, scratch that last line, because you have to be willing and motivated to actually take action and make this stuff work for you.

And in all honesty, I don't know what kind of person you are or if you are able to follow through on the things you put your mind to, so I can't guarantee that what this book teaches will work for everyone, but I can guarantee that it will at the very least give you the knowledge and insight you need so that you know what to do if you ever decide to get around to it.

Like if you're determined to just learn these secrets and not actually do anything with them, then of course they won't work for you, because you reap what you sow. And if you sow nothing, well then you can't really expect to gain anything. But if you are willing to actually make an effort, take action, and put the secrets you learn here to work, then there really isn't anything else you'll ever need to learn about doing well with women ever again, because you'll know exactly what to do.

CHAPTER 1
ROCK BOTTOM

BEFORE WE DELVE into the material, I think it's best that you understand a little about myself and my background.

My name is Zephaniah Netz, call me Zeph, I graduated uni with an accounting degree and got a job for a big accounting firm. I was fairly successful at my work, as successful as an accountant could be. Though I was never good with women.

When I was 25 years old I started to get massively depressed. I mean, here I was, a man with a bachelor's degree, in my mid-twenties, and I had no idea how I would ever find a partner in life. I was lost with no idea of what to do. However, I had too much of an ego to admit that it was my own fault for not figuring out what to do about it.

So what did I do? I ignored the problem. I ignored the problem for 10 more years. I told myself I should just focus on my job and make more money, and that if I did that, then eventually the perfect woman for me would just come into my life.

So what happened? Well, 10 years later, I was still an accountant, and I had gotten two raises in my salary, so I was financially a bit better off. However, I was 35 years old now, and far more depressed now than when I was 25, as well as developed a pot belly, and I'd never had a girlfriend. And actually, to be honest, I had never even been on a real date.

One night alone in my apartment, I broke down and cried at a loss of where I had gone wrong in my life. I didn't see how things could get any better. I thought to myself, *I've missed my twenties, I lost my chance, I'm old now, and now it's too late for me, I'll never get married, I'll never have kids, I'll never be happy, what is the point of life?*

I had many thoughts of ending my life, seeing no point, not seeing any kind of bright future for myself. I felt stuck, I felt trapped, and I didn't see any hope. I now knew what rock bottom felt like, because that was exactly where I was. Though it's really true what they say that once you hit rock bottom, there is nowhere to go but up from there, because in those most painful moments with myself, with tears streaming down my face, I admitted to myself that I knew nothing about women, that I had been a fool my whole life.

I was too much of a coward to actually end my life, though it was too painful to continue living my life as I had been living it, which was going to work every day, eating a drive-through breakfast, eating lunch alone, eating dinners alone, spending weekends walking around aimlessly often in tears. I'd go to places like malls on the weekends, where people were, so I could feel like I was with others, but I felt so completely alone. And I'd escape my sadness, for just a moment, by stepping into the cafe at the mall and ordering their largest-size frappuccino. That wonderful sugar high was the only thing that would make me forget, even if just for a short time, how terrible my life had become.

I looked at myself in the mirror in tears and told myself, "You've been lying to yourself all this time, Zeph, you don't know jack about women! Look at yourself Zeph, you're on the brink of suicide here," then screaming at myself, "Zeph, you can't do this anymore! Zeph, put the knife down! You're going to make a change! Because your job from this point on is not accounting anymore, it's learning about women, learning all the stuff you've missed out on over the years, it's time to catch up on what you've missed."

CHAPTER 2
APPROACH ANXIETY

THE NEXT DAY, I woke up, went to work, and the whole work day I felt extremely excited, looking forward to the end of the day when I'd get out of work, because I knew exactly what I was going to do the moment I got home, which was to get on my laptop and start learning about women.

The work day went slow, but the moment 5 pm rolled around, I ran for my car, went through a drive-thru to grab dinner, sped home, and was able to make it to my one-bedroom apartment by 5:30 pm, looking forward to working on what seemed to be the most important research project of my life.

As I took a bite of my burger, I typed into the search bar, "How to get a girlfriend." And I wasn't ready for what came up, which were tons of search results, mostly articles. I started clicking on each link on the first page, going from top to bottom, and read what was there, and what I found was that each piece of information seemed to contradict the other pieces of information I had read. And after reading lots of conflicting pieces of information, I soon realized that I wasn't going to find the answers I wanted here.

It was then that I noticed an ad. The ad said, "No more

lonely nights, learn the secrets of attracting women, and meet the women of your dreams."

Wow, I thought to myself, this company has promised everything I've ever wanted to know. And so I clicked on the ad, which brought me to another page with even more information on it. As I read further, I soon realized what they were selling here, they were selling a pickup artist bootcamp with a pickup artist master who would train me in the art of attraction, and it was only four thousand dollars for a whole weekend of training, and came with a money-back guarantee.

How lucky I had to be to have stumbled upon this ad. It must be fate. I was destined to have clicked this ad, and learn the real secrets of meeting women from a pro. So without thinking, I had gotten out my credit card, paid, and scheduled my bootcamp for this coming weekend.

I was ecstatic, thinking that this was going to solve all of my problems.

The week went by quickly, and I felt super pumped, and when Friday rolled around, I felt so happy and excited that my life was about to change forever.

As soon as 5 pm hit, I bolted out of work, hopped in my car, and quickly drove to a steak house, the place the email I'd received said I was to meet the pickup artist master who would be training me.

When I arrived in the parking lot, I got out of the car and called the number from the email, and a guy answered, "Hello, is this Zeph?" a voice said.

"Yes, that's me."

"Good, good, are you at the spot?"

"Yes, I'm here."

"I see you, I'll be right over in a minute."

The phone clicked, and I looked around, my heart was pounding so hard, I was nervous but totally excited to meet the man who would change my life.

A little thin man popped up with curly bright red hair, a

freckled face, and deep green eyes, he must have been about five foot seven. I'm six foot one, so he was much smaller than myself.

"Hey there Zeph!" he said, "the name's, John, nice to meet you."

"Hi, I said," shaking his hand.

"Well, let's go get some steaks and we'll get started."

"Sure."

I followed him into the steak house. It was a dimly lit place, they had a bar at one end, and a large section with tables at the other end.

John mumbled something to the wait staff and we were quickly seated.

We both scanned the menu for a short while, and our waitress came over and we both ordered.

Then John started, "So you're a lucky man Zeph, because I usually do these boot camps with 3 to 4 students at a time, but you're the only one this weekend, so you lucked out, because it means I can focus all of my energy on you."

"Wow! That's great!" I was so happy that I had gotten lucky, and so the whole bootcamp would be focused entirely on me.

"So tell me Zeph, how much experience have you had with women?"

"Well, to be honest, none."

"You've never had a girlfriend?"

"No, I haven't," I said, "that's why I'm here, I want a girl-friend. Could you do that? Could you help me get a girlfriend?"

"Oh, that's easy!"

Just then our steaks arrived and we started eating. As we ate, John explained that we'd be meeting women tonight after dinner, and that tomorrow we'd be meeting more women, and that Sunday we'd be meeting even more women.

I didn't realize we'd be meeting women tonight, I started

feeling a bit nervous. I didn't realize we'd be meeting women tomorrow or the next day either.

"So do you have any questions for me?" John asked.

"Ah, well, I was just wondering, where will we be meeting women tonight?" I asked back.

"Right over there," John said as he pointed over to the bar.

I started feeling really nervous now, "Right over there, at that bar?" I asked, just to make sure I understood him correctly.

"Yup, that's right."

I noticed John had just finished his plate and I had a few more bites left, and my heart was pounding. I hadn't realized we'd be meeting women so fast. I expected some kind of preparatory training for this, so I asked, "Um … how exactly will we be meeting women? I mean like, how will this work?"

"Ah, I understand, basically after we're done eating, we'll pay the bill, and then we'll go to the bar, and each grab a drink, and see what kind of ladies are there. And you tell me if there's one you like, and then you're going to walk up to her and talk to her. Don't worry though, you'll be fine, I won't let you drown, I'll coach you through the whole thing."

I thought it was kind of him not to let me drown, as I ate my last bite.

John signaled to the waitress, and she came, and we split the bill. I felt like it was a bit odd that I had paid 4K already for this bootcamp and still had to split the bill over meals, perhaps it's something I had missed in the terms.

"Okay, it's game time," John said as he stood up, "but don't worry, it's going to be fine, you've got this."

I stood up and followed John to the bar, trying to keep myself from shaking out of nervousness.

When we got to the bar, I noticed there were a lot of women here, sitting in groups on stools at tall tables drinking and talking away.

"Two beers," John said to the bartender, slipping him a bill, and then passed me a beer.

How nice of this man to buy me a beer after I paid 4 grand for this, I thought.

"So have a look around the room, see any women you like?"

As I looked around, my jaw dropped, I had a hard time finding a woman I didn't like, but there was one in particular, a blond wearing a black tank top and jeans, who was sitting on a stool talking to another woman who must have been her friend. "I like that one," I said to John, "the one with the blond hair wearing the black tank top and jeans."

"Well, that's great! Go talk to her."

"Wha, what? I don't know what to do. I don't know what to say."

"Tell her, 'Wow! I'm impressed with the way you style your hair. You're a talented one, aren't you?' Okay?"

"Yes, I've got it!"

"Repeat it back to me."

"Wow! I'm impressed with the way you style your hair. You're a talented one, aren't you?"

"One more time, and try to match my tone and slight sarcasm, 'Wow! I'm impressed with the way you style your hair. You're a talented one, aren't you?.'"

"Wow! I'm impressed with the way you style your hair. You're a talented one, aren't you?"

"Perfect, let's go talk to them."

"Wait, but what do I say after that?"

"She'll likely talk, but if not, then I'll help you out, sound good?"

"Yeah, I think so."

"Oh, one more thing, move your beer away from your chest, and instead hold it lower, by your side, and keep your shoulders straight."

I lowered my beer and held it to my side and moved my shoulders backwards a little. "Like this?"

John then stood in front of me looking into my eyes and then looking me over from my eyes down to my shoes and then back up to my eyes, "Let me see a smile," John said with a smile on his face.

I smiled.

"Perfect! I want you to try to hold that smile, come on, we're going in," John said as he pushed me in front of him in the direction of the 2 women.

We were halfway there, and my heart kept beating louder and louder, I could hear it, and I froze, I couldn't do it, I couldn't take another step forward.

John, pushing me from behind said, "What are you doing? Just go up to her and say the line we just rehearsed."

I turned around to face John, "I can't."

"You can't, what do you mean you can't?"

"I don't know, I just can't"

"No, no, no, no, no, you can't do this, it's an act of self-sabotage. You're doing a disservice to yourself by not walking up to that woman and saying your line."

"I can't remember my line."

"I see, you know what this means?"

"No, what does it mean?"

"It means your problem is far worse than I had previously imagined."

"So what do I do?"

"You sure you can't just go forward a few more feet and just say, 'Hi' to her?"

"I can't."

"Okay, don't worry, I've seen this before, it happens to the best of us, it's what we in the pickup community call approach anxiety, just means we need to work on your confidence a little."

"How do we do that?"

Some people were pushing to get around us, and some other people were singing happy birthday to someone just a few feet away, it was hard to hear.

"Let's go over there to that corner and talk further over the rest of our beers," John said, pointing to a corner far in the back with no people there.

"Okay!" I said as I followed his lead.

We zig-zagged through the crowd and made it to the spot.

John, facing me, put his hand on my shoulder, and looked me deep in the eye, "Let me tell you something."

"I'm listening."

"You know what happens when you don't approach a woman you like quickly?"

"No, what happens?"

"Another man will approach her, he'll take her home, tomorrow he'll be her boyfriend, and in two years they'll be married. Is that what you want?!"

"No, I don't want that."

"Look at that woman you wanted to talk to, do you see her, another man started talking to her already. Maybe you'll have another chance, or maybe it's over."

"Really? What? Oh my god! Yes, I see her, you're right, another man is talking to her."

"Look Zeph, I used to be like you, so innocent, so gullible, weak! I was fucking weak! And I used to have the worst fear of approaching women, the thought of approaching a woman made my whole body tremble with fear."

"So how did you fix it."

"You can't fix it, but I'll tell you what helped me."

"What helped you."

"I realized something."

"What did you realize?"

"You see John, thousands of years ago, us men, we used to face life or death situations every day, if we wanted to eat we had to hunt, and hunting was a life or death situation, because we didn't have guns back then like we have now, we had sticks and stones, and some animals could easily kill us if we made one wrong move. And if we wanted to meet a woman so that we could reproduce, we had to approach them and talk to them, which was also a life or death situation, because if we approached the wrong woman, another man could kill us. Our genes want us to eat, it's why food smells and tastes so good, and our genes want us to approach women so we can reproduce, it's why we're attracted to them. Get it?"

"Yes, I get it."

"But now, society has brainwashed us, made us weak, put us in cubicles, in chairs in cushy little jobs, in box-shaped apartments, and makes it easy for us to buy our food. And that's fine and all, it's a good exchange for what society gives us, we don't have to risk our lives to eat. And because society employs police, we don't have to risk our lives anymore when we want to approach and talk to a woman, because no one will murder us over an approach, I mean it can happen technically, but it's rare. However, the fear of the approach still exists. The reason you're so nervous is because you fear death, but death is extremely unlikely to happen. The worst that would happen is that the woman would simply tell you to go away."

"That makes a lot of sense, John, but what can I do about it?"

"You need to realize that this is a life and death situation for you!"

"What?"

"I mean, if you see a woman you like and if you don't at least approach her and at least introduce yourself, you're genes will die off, you'll never reproduce, never have any offspring to carry on your legacy, and your entire lineage, all the people who lived and died, suffered sweat and tears, to produce every single human in your bloodline will have suffered in vain, because that bloodline ends with you. Essentially what I'm saying is when you fail to approach a woman you're attracted to you're not only failing yourself but your failing all the people who came before you. So the next time you see a woman you're interested in and you don't approach, you're letting down generations of people who survived wars, famines, pandemics, and all manner of atrocities for the sole purpose of putting you here now so you could make the approach when the chance arose to do so. By not approaching, you're basically saying your life and their lives are all meaningless, that it was all pointless, that everything your ancestors fought for to be able to get to the point to produce you was for nothing. Is that what you want, Zeph? Are you going to let all those generations of your ancestors down like that, because you're so comfortable in your cushy little job, with your pre-prepared meals, and your frappuccinos, that you would disrespect the very reason you were put on this Earth, and end your bloodline right here, today, because you couldn't handle that little bit of fear that comes with making the approach? All you're ancestors handled their fear and made the approach, and as for you? What are you going to do Zeph?"

"Oh my god, I had never thought of it like that. That's not what I want, I don't want to let all those people down, I'm sorry, I'm sorry." I suddenly exploded into tears. John had really gotten to me, I wasn't mentally prepared for everything he had just said. I started to feel guilty for thinking he was cheap by not paying for my meal, this wonderful man here, John, the man who had just shared with me the purpose of my life, something no one else had ever told me, was my savior. I started to see John in a completely different light, he was more than a mere pickup artist master, he was the wisest man I had ever met, he was a genius, he was god!

Still sobbing, I said, "I don't want to let them down, I'll do it, I will make the approach, I will conquer my fear!"

"What will you conquer? Say it again?"

"I will conquer my fear!"

"Again!"

"I will conquer my fear!"

"Louder!"

"I will conquer my fear!"

"Good."

"But how can I conquer my fear, John?"

"Simple, the next time you see a woman you think you might like, you remember your ancestors, and you remember that the meaning of your very existence will be destroyed if you give into your fear, if you fail to approach, if you let your ancestors down. Capeesh?"

"Capeesh!"

"Good! Looks like we're making progress, next round is on you," John said as he downed the rest of his beer.

Damned, I knew there was a catch to him buying me that beer, I thought to myself as I gulped down the rest of my beer.

"Okay, back to the bar Zeph, and call me 'Sensei' from now on."

"Yes, Sensei," I said as I led the way back to the bar.

Those few minutes walking back to the bar I realized, this man John was a blessing, he had already changed my life in so many ways by revealing my purpose. I had never had a purpose before, and now I had one. It was only the beginning of the night, and already I had been touched, deeply moved by this wonderful man, John, a man I couldn't feel more proud to call my Sensei.

CHAPTER 3
FIERCE REJECTION

AT THE BAR, I ordered John and myself another beer, and when the bartender put the beers down on the bar, I paid and we each grabbed our beers and took a sip.

"Look around again, and tell me if you see a woman you like," John said.

I scanned the room, and then I saw her, a beautiful brunette wearing cat eye sunglasses, a silver chain link necklace, a beige crop top, and white cargo pants, standing alone at a table sipping on what appeared to be a glass of red wine. "That one," I said, motioning towards her direction with my head, "the one with the cat eye sunglasses and beige crop top."

"Whoah, nice choice! That's what I'm talking about."

"So, what do I do?"

"Well, you're going to have to talk to her. Hmmm… since she's alone, you're going to have to approach her alone."

"But what do I say? And then what do I say after that? And after that? I'm nervous as fuck, but I just have no idea what to say."

"Well, you're in luck Zeph, because you hired the best bootcamp instructor in the business. Come here, let me show you something," John said, as he pulled a small white case out of his pocket that he quickly unzipped. John then took a small black thing out of the case that he clipped to the collar of my shirt, "This is your microphone," and took out a second black thing that he affixed to my ear, "And this is your earphone."

Then he put one on his shirt collar and one in his ear.

"Can you hear me Zeph?"

"Oh my god, that's amazing Sensei. Haha! Yes, I hear you loud and clear!"

"So remember your ancestors, your great great great great great great great granddad wasn't afraid when he had to fight that lion so he could survive and later approach that woman he was interested in, and so his offspring could be born starting a line of humans leading up to you. You need to respect him and approach this woman now! Because if you don't approach her, you'll be responsible for the non-existence of all the humans that would have came after you! Although you're nervous, there are no lions here, and you won't actually be killed by anyone for making an approach, since we're in a restaurant and there's security all around and all. And anyway, I'll be able to hear the whole conversation, so I'll tell you what to say if you get into trouble. Now go approach her quickly, before another man does, and compliment something about her clothing, hmmm… compliment her sunglasses, just look her in the eyes and say, 'Cool shades, I'm Zeph,' and then put out your hand like you want to shake her hand. Other than that, try to come up with what to say on your own at first, I want to see how you do, but don't worry because if you ever freeze, I'll tell you the perfect words."

"Yes, Sensei." This was amazing, John really did come prepared for this. I felt so lucky to have such a good Sensei.

I started to walk in her direction, my heart was beating hard. I started to feel extremely nervous. I felt like I was going to faint, but I couldn't let my ancestors down, they had all died to put me here in the shoes I'm in now, I have to succeed on this one, I have to do it for them. "For my ancestors!" I said to myself.

I was so scared that I was shaking, with each step my legs felt like they were getting heavier. Thousands of voices in my head were saying, "Turn back now, don't approach, this is ridiculous son, what are you doing? You're going to approach and she's going to reject you!" And I froze.

I could hear a voice in my head saying, "Zeph! Zeph! Zeph! Zeph!"

It seemed like each iteration of the voice was getting louder. I wondered, was this my inner voice talking to me? Perhaps my subconscious. Maybe it's my ancestors. "Hello ancestors, are you there?"

"No Zeph, this is not your inner voice or your subconscious, it's not your ancestors either, it's you're fucking Sensei! And you look like a fool right now standing in the middle of a crowd talking to yourself!"

"Ah. I remember now. I'm approaching a woman, and you're my Sensei."

"Yes Zeph, good! You're approaching a woman and I'm you're Sensei, Jesus fucking Christ! Get ahold of yourself, man! Focus! You need to approach this woman and compliment her sunglasses and introduce yourself, you're almost there, just a few more steps. Do it! Do it now! For your ancestors! Don't worry man, I got your back! Just move forward and speak to her! You got this! And stop looking up at the ceiling, focus your eyes on her! You can't approach her if you're not focusing on her, please, focus on her!"

"Yes Sensei, I'm looking at her now, I'm focusing on her."

"And remember to put one foot in front of the other so you can get to her."

"Oh right, putting one foot in front of the other, oh my god, I'm getting closer, I'm getting closer, it's working Sensei, it's working! Ha ha ha! I think I'm in front of her now, I think I made it!"

"Zeph, focus! Look at her and compliment her sunglasses!"

"Oh right!"

"Are you on the phone?" a voice said.

"Is that you Sensei?"

"Who's Sensei?"

"Are you my ancestors?"

"Why did you just walk to my table?"

"Look at her, Zeph!"

"Oh right, Sensei."

I turned my head, and there she was. "She's even more gorgeous up close than I had imagined seeing her from afar."

"What?" the woman said.

I looked her in the eyes, "Oh, um … I meant…"

"Compliment her sunglasses Zeph!"

"Okay, shut up for a moment, I can't focus with all these voices talking to me at once, I'm trying, I'm trying my fucking best!"

"What?" the woman said again with a shocked look on her face.

"Um … sorry, I meant those sunglasses you have on, they're quite amazing!" I said.

"Thank you, and who were you talking to, what voices?"

"Oh, nothing, just my ancestors," I said, being at a loss for words and still feeling quite nervous.

"Ancestors? Do you mean ghosts? Wait, you're not psychic, are you? I love the paranormal."

"I can't say what I mean right now, but I love the paranormal too."

"Tell her your name!"

"By the way, my name's Zeph."

"And put out your hand to shake her hand!"

"I'm so happy to meet you Zeph, call me Jackie," the

woman said shaking my hand, "you know it's such a relief to meet you Zeph, given all the creeps and weirdos in this place."

"'Jackie,' that's such a nice name, it's an honor to finally meet you."

"Wait, what do you mean, 'finally meet me,'" Jackie quickly snapped back as one of her eyebrows raised.

"Oh, I mean I was trying to get to you for a while now, from the bar way over there."

"You're giving her too much information, Zeph."

"What do you mean, 'trying to get to me for a while?'"

"Oh, I just mean when I saw you, I knew I had to talk to you, but I felt scared."

"You're giving her too much information again, Zeph."

"No man has ever told me anything like that before, do go on, what do you mean you felt scared?"

"I mean just what I said, I felt scared."

"I see," Jackie said seeming to be a bit irritated.

I didn't know what to say to that, I felt like the mood suddenly became awkward.

"Well, Mr. Zeph, why exactly did you feel scared? Do you think I'm going to bite you?" Jackie said with a giggle.

"Um … no, I wasn't implying that at all, it's just that I've never talked to a woman before, I mean like this."

Both of her eyes widened.

"I mean, I never approached and talked to a woman before in this kind of situation, or actually, in any kind of situation."

"You're giving her too much information yet again, Zeph."

"Well, I do like your honesty, Zeph, it's so rare to meet a truly honest man these days," Jackie said, now looking deep into my eyes with a smile on her face.

"Wow, Zeph, you've got this handled, doing good!"

"So, Zeph, now that you can see that there's nothing to

fear, and we've finally met, what oh what do you intend to do with me?"

"That's a good question, I actually hadn't thought that far ahead about it."

"Tell her to leave with you, Zeph."

"Jackie, I feel comfortable talking to you, I'd never met a woman I feel comfortable talking to, I like that, how about let's get out of this place together?"

"Where would we go, Zeph?"

"That's a good question, I hadn't thought about that either, but I'm sure we'll figure it out," I said smiling. I smiled because I didn't know what else to do.

"Oh my god, Zeph, you're a natural with words, you definitely don't need my help to talk to the ladies, you've got this!"

She smiled back, and said, "Are you able to drive?"

I actually, wasn't sure I was able to drive. I mean, given the fact I barely made it to this table to talk to this lady, and given the fact that I completely forgot what I was going to say and I thought my ancestors were talking to me. But she was looking at me, I had to answer, so I looked her in the eye and smiled and said, "I think so!" I'll always remember to never say that again, because that's when everything started to go sour.

"You think so? What the fuck does that mean, 'you think so?' How could you just say that with that snarky smile? I was so wrong about you. Uggh!" Jackie said as she rolled her eyes.

"Wait, let me explain."

"Don't talk to me! Get the fuck out of my face!"

"Zeph, abort mission!"

"No, wait."

"I said, get the fuck out of my face!" Jackie said, emptying her wine glass on my face, and then picking up a handful of nuts out of the small wooden nut bowl on the table and throwing them at my face screaming at the top of her lungs now so the whole bar could hear, "I said, get the fuck out of my face, you fucking jerk!"

"Zeph, get out of there!"

I turned around and quickly walked away from her. She seemed so welcoming at first, I couldn't imagine what had gotten into her to set her off like that. Maybe she thought I was too drunk and not able to drive.

I walked straight through the crowd towards John, when suddenly a bouncer grabbed my right arm from behind, "Sir, I'm going to have to ask you to leave."

"But I didn't do anything!" I said, turning around to face the bouncer.

"Sir, I'm sorry, but you have to leave right now or we're going to have to call the police."

"Zeph, just do what he says and I'll meet you outside," John said.

"Okay, Okay, I understand, I'll leave," I said to the bouncer.

He was a big guy, about two inches taller than me and more heavy set with thig muscular arms. He walked with me all the way to the exit holding my right arm.

"Sorry sir," he said when we got to the door, "but if you had listened to the lady the first time she rejected you, you could have stayed. Continuing to talk to someone when your presence isn't welcome is harassment, and we have a zero-tolerance policy for it. If you're too drunk to drive, I would suggest calling a cab to take you home. We, unfortunately, can't have you hanging around the door because we don't want you harassing any of the other customers, so you have 10 minutes to get lost."

Just then John popped through the door, "Hey my man, you okay?" John said, coming over to me.

"I told him he has 10 minutes to leave, if he's your friend

you might want to drive him home, because based on his behavior in there, I'd guess he's had too much to drink."

"Yes, sir, I'll get him home, apologies for this."

Then, John put his arm around me, "Don't worry bud, we'll go elsewhere."

It was still early, only around 8:30, I couldn't believe I got kicked out of that place so early, and I didn't even do anything wrong, except maybe say the wrong thing.

"We're going to go across the street, they have a good little restaurant there known for their ice cream sundaes, it's usually dead around this time. We'll grab some dessert and coffee there, and talk about what happened, and about our plan for tomorrow."

CHAPTER 4
REAL TALK

ME AND JOHN sat across from each other at a little table in the small restaurant working on our ice cream sundaes.

"I told you to get out of there, why did you continue trying to talk to her?"

"Well, she had been so nice to me, and I couldn't understand why she suddenly wanted me gone."

"Why do you think she wanted you gone?"

"I think it's because I didn't seem sure as to whether I could drive."

"You're totally right, good you realize that. So if you could go back in time, what could you have done better?"

"I could have told her, 'I don't think I can drive right now, could I get your number and we go out another time?'"

"That's good you realize now what you should have done, but it's too late for that now. Perhaps this is my fault, I didn't realize that just two beers would have messed you up so much. At first, I thought it was just your anxiety and not the alcohol, but now I'm thinking that probably it was a combination of both. New Rule: You are no longer allowed to drink alcohol."

"But alcohol helped with my anxiety, it calmed me a little in a situation where I was nervous."

"No, no more alcohol for you Zeph, you're going to have to conquer your anxiety without it, alcohol is a crutch, it doesn't really help you. If you hadn't been drinking, it might have been you and her sitting here together having ice cream sundaes instead of you and me."

"You're right, Sensei."

"Look Zeph, tomorrow I'm taking you to do something else called day game. And actually, from now on, I recommend that day game is all you do, no more nights out at bars, at least for the time being, okay?"

"Yes, I'm okay with that."

"Good, so anyway, I think you're actually a good talker, you don't need me to tell you what to say once you get yourself into a conversation with a woman, because you were doing just fine once you had the courage to approach, rather you need me to help you to do approaches in the first place, until you get the hang of it. Would you agree?"

"Yeah, you're right, I agree."

"Good. So tomorrow, do you know where we're going to go?"

"I have no idea, where will we go?"

"To the train station!"

"What? But why? What's there? Will we take a train somewhere?"

"You'll find out tomorrow. For the moment though, I want to share with you the real secrets of attraction, and what actually would make a woman want to be with you. Do you have any idea what would attract a woman to a man?"

"Yeah, I think it's all about looks and money, if I look like a model and have a billion dollars, then I'd easily attract any woman."

"You know, Zeph, that's what nearly every man says to me when I ask the same question. However, if it was really all about looks and money, then does that mean that poor men who don't look like models would never have a chance of getting a girlfriend or getting married?"

"Yeah, they would never have a chance of getting a girl-friend or getting married."

"Okay, let's assume you're right about that. Then answer me this, does your dad look like a model?"

"Actually, no he doesn't."

"And is your dad rich?"

"Actually, no he isn't."

"So how is it he married your mom?"

"Well, hmmm, I'm not sure exactly, but I think things were different back then."

"Okay, maybe things were different back then. Well, do you know anyone who has a girlfriend or is married that doesn't look like a model and is not rich?"

"Now that I think about it … Yes, the majority of my friends are all married and none of them look anything like a model or make anything more than an average guy."

"And would you consider the wives or girlfriends of your friends to be good-looking?"

"Come to think of it, yes, nearly all of my friends either have a beautiful girlfriend or a beautiful wife."

"So why is it that all of them succeeded, but you failed?"

"You know, that's something I've been asking myself almost every day since graduating college, and I really don't know, I just thought I never met the right person yet. Maybe they got lucky and met the right person and I didn't."

"Yes, Zeph, I totally agree with you, what it's actually more about is having the opportunity to meet the right person. You see, with what we're going to be doing tomorrow with day game is we're going to be putting the odds of meeting the right person in your favor. As long as you are motivated to meet the right person, it's pretty much impos-sible that you won't."

"Really?"

"Pretty much. All that is required from you is to maintain a positive attitude, an open mind, and the motivation to keep trying. Are you able to maintain those three things?"

"Yeah, I should have no problem maintaining those three things."

"Then you're going to be just fine, because as long as you're able to maintain those three things, there is no way you won't be successful at finding the right woman for you, make sure you remember that. In fact, to be honest, those three things are the entire secret to meeting women. It's, in fact, so obvious what is needed to do well with women that most guys completely overlook it."

"Just a moment, John, I will write down those three things in my phone, so I don't forget them."

"Sure, write it down."

"Wrote it."

"Do you feel okay to drive now? I think you've only had 2 beers over a span of 2 hours, and it's been over an hour now since you finished your last beer and got kicked out of that last restaurant, which means you've got to be completely sober now."

"Yes, I actually feel completely sober."

"Well, let's order a coffee and spend 30 more minutes here just to make sure, and then I'm going to give you a sobriety test, and if you pass, after that you're going to go home, and you're going to get up 6 am, because I'll be at your place at 7 am to pick you up."

"That sounds great, John."

"Awesome!"

CHAPTER 5
APPROACHES

I WOKE up to my alarm blaring at 6 am. John would be here soon, so I scrambled to shit, shower, and shave. Then got dressed, nuked and wolfed down a ham and cheese hot pocket for breakfast, and was ready to go.

It was 6:40 am now, so I had twenty minutes left to kill. Checked the note in my phone that read, "Maintain a positive attitude, an open mind, and the motivation to keep trying." Yup, I had all of those things, I was set!

Then I thought for a few minutes about what to do, and then remembered, I need a coffee.

Made an instant coffee, black, and drank it down. Only ten minutes left until seven, what to do?

I did a bunch of pushups, then a bunch of situps, it was almost time. So I walked out the front door, locked it behind me, ran down the stairs of my apartment building, and waited on the front porch staring at the street.

It was 7 am now, and where was John? He said he'd be here, what if he decided not to come?

Just then a blue Corvette pulled into the complex parking lot, drove around, and pulled up to the porch, it was John.

I went down the 2 steps of the porch and saw John make a motion with his hand for me to hop in, so I hopped in.

John looked at me and smiled, "Hey bud," he said, and we were off, out of the complex and onto the main road.

John then took an exit onto the highway, and I actually had no idea where we were going, I had never been to the train station before. I mean, I always drive everywhere, who even takes the train nowadays?

In about ten minutes, John took an exit off the highway and then turned into this huge parking lot, it was probably the biggest parking lot I had ever seen in my life. This must be the train station.

John parked somewhere on the outskirts of the parking lot where there were barely any cars, then seemed to be paying some fee on an app on his phone. Why is he paying his bills now?

"Let's go," John said as he opened his door.

I opened my door and followed him.

As we walked through the parking lot, the number of parked cars as well as cars driving around looking for a parking space seemed to increase. Made sense why he chose to park on the outskirts of this huge parking lot.

I then noticed this huge building far off in the distance which we were walking towards.

When we finally got to the building there were people everywhere outside, many walking in and out of the entrance doors and some just hanging out outside in various groups.

"Come on," John said, "we're going inside."

I followed him through the entrance doors, and the place looked like a mall.

"We're not here to catch a train," John said, "we're here to check out the scene, if you catch my drift."

I honestly had no idea what he was talking about, but just looked at him and smiled and nodded to be polite.

John walked into a small alley between two cafes, in front

of a big main walkway, and then put his arm around me while looking at the main walkway.

"Why did we stop?" I asked, "What are we doing?"

"You see all these people walking by? I want you to sift through the crowds with your eyes and find a woman that you'd like to get to know better."

"What? What do you mean? Why?"

"Because the moment you find one that catches your eye, you're going to approach her and try to find out more about her."

"What?" My heart started to pound at the thought of talking to a woman who I didn't know. I was frightened.

"You scared?"

"Yes, very."

"Good, you should be scared, you wouldn't be a cool dude if you weren't scared. Anyway, don't worry, you don't have to approach any women if you don't want to. You can just sift through the crowd all day with your eyes if it makes you feel comfortable, it's all up to you."

That made me feel tons better knowing that I wouldn't have to approach any women if I didn't want to. Of course, I didn't want to. I totally had the best Sensei in the world, allowing me to not approach anyone.

"I just want you to look around, and just let me know if you see anyone you like, no need to even think about approaching them. Think of it as simply an exercise in being able to spot women you might be into from a distance."

I looked around and saw this extremely cute, petite woman with straight jet-black hair and glasses, wearing a black leather jacket, a black T-shirt that said, 'Anarchy' in red letters, and blue ripped jeans.

"Her," I said, "in the black leather jacket with the Anarchy shirt and blue jeans."

"That's great, so I have a question for you, what happens

if you don't approach quickly?" John asked in a soft, slow tone.

"Well, she'll probably get on a train, and I'll never see her again."

"You are correct, but what did you learn last night during my lesson?" John asked, again in a soft, slow tone.

"Another man will approach her, and tomorrow he'll become her boyfriend, and in two years they'll get married," I said gleefully, knowing that it was the right answer. John couldn't put one over on me, I knew my stuff.

"Correct again," John said in a slow and soft tone yet again.

This new slow and soft tone he was sporting was getting creepy, just what was his point?

"But what happens to you if you don't approach her? Remember your ancestors?"

"If I don't approach her, I'll never reproduce, and my genes will die off, and I will have destroyed everything my ancestors went through to put me here in this situation now," I said smugly.

"Correct again," John said yet again in a slow and soft tone, and then silence.

I thought for a second as visions of my ancestors dying in wars and surviving pandemics came to mind. Fuck! John did put one over on me, I have to approach, because if I don't my lineage ends here.

Suddenly my heart began to pound, I felt like a nervous wreck, but could hear John's voice in my head, 'Put one foot in front of the other.' And so I started to do that, moving forward as I put one foot in front of the other.

"That's it, man! Put one foot in front of the other and make this approach, you've got this!" I could hear John say. As I looked back I saw him smiling as he gave me a wink.

I have to do this, I have to talk to her, my ancestors are

depending on me. But what do I say to her when I get to her? And why does my heart keep pounding? That's right, it's the fear of death. Wait, I remember, I need to compliment something about her, a piece of clothing, her 'Anarchy' shirt, I'll compliment that.

Now knowing what to say, I felt a little boost of confidence, though it was ever so slight, barely noticeable. Who am I kidding? I have no confidence. I looked to my left and she was there now, right beside me.

"I don't want to kill off my offspring, I don't want to disappoint my ancestors!"

"Who are you talking to? I'm right here?" a voice said.

"Who was that? Was it my ancestors?"

"Doing good, just keep your shoulders parallel to hers like you're doing, look to your left using your head and neck, but don't turn your body, and say your opening line," I could hear John say from behind me, seemingly not caring if she heard him or not.

I looked to my left being careful to use just my head and neck, keeping my shoulders parallel to hers like John said. As I turned my head, she was looking right into my eyes. My jaw dropped.

"I dig your T-shirt," I said, "Anarchy is so cool!"

I actually prefer capitalism, I thought to myself. But wait, I wonder if her T-shirt means she's literally into anarchy or if it's the name of a musical artist.

"Wow! You like Anarchy too?" She said.

"I do!" I said, still not knowing if her t-shirt really meant literal anarchy or not, "But wait, it's weird us meeting here, like this, both into the same thing. We should talk more."

"Yeah," she said, "I'm Sara, what's your name?"

"Hi Sara, my name is Zeph," I said, still walking with her, trying to match her speed. What do I say next?

"Zeph is quite a unique name, I like it."

I almost froze, and then it came to me, "Hey, you want to grab a coffee?"

"I can't right now, I'm on the way to class."

"Well, then let me get your number."

"Oh, sure," she said, then flipped to a screen on her phone with her number and handed it to me.

"Just a moment," I said, "I'm adding you." I quickly added her and then texted her, "Zeph here," then passed her back her phone.

She wrote something in her phone, and suddenly I got a text, "Nice to meet you Zeph, text me later," the text said.

Receiving that text, I felt amazing, I felt the best I had ever felt in my life.

"I will," I said verbally with a smile.

"This is my gate, gotta go now," she said with a smile as she went through the gate.

I waved, and she waved back.

I felt so absolutely incredible! And when I turned around, John was there.

"So Zeph, you got your first number I see, and quite surprised that no woman has really rejected you yet, immediately after your approach anyway, I mean. You've got some skills Zeph, not even sure why you ever needed to hire me."

"No Sensei, I've never done this type of stuff in my life, I owe it all to you. Before I met you, I never got any woman's number before."

"Well, let's see if you can keep up your streak, look around now and find another one you like."

"Um… okay." I started to look around again, it was really crowded in the spot we were in, people everywhere. I scanned the place sifting through all the different people. And then I saw her, this beautiful woman, with short brown hair, glasses, and blue eyes, wearing green trousers, a green coat with a white blouse underneath, and carrying a black purse over her shoulder. "That one, over there in the green coat."

"Well, go on over and see what she's about."

"Will do!" I said looking John in the eye, then started walking through the crowd towards her, my eyes hawk-like, fixated on her. I noticed my heart wasn't beating as fast as before, I wasn't nervous anymore, was I cured of my anxiety? I felt amazing.

I moved in by her side, walking right next to her, our shoulders parallel to each other, and then turned my head saying, "I like that coat."

She didn't turn her head, didn't respond, she was completely ignoring me. "Hey, I like your coat!" I said a little louder.

"I heard you the first time. I was purposely ignoring you because I'm married with five kids," she said, lifting up her hand to show me the wedding band on her finger, "but I'm flattered you came over here to try to start a conversation with me. Anyway, see you."

Feeling a bit let down, I stopped and turned around to look for John, who soon popped up in front of me.

"Find the next one," John said.

Again, I looked around, and saw in the distance, a tall woman with dark black hair, wearing shutter shades. She had these big hoop earrings, white pants, a white shirt, a white jacket, and nicely shaped curves. "That one, in all white with the shutter shades," I said.

"Well, you know what to do," John said.

"I sure do," I said, and then proceeded to approach the woman.

I approached her head-on looking her straight in the eyes, saying, "Wow! I like those shades."

She dodged to my left side and passed by me, saying nothing. I stood there for a moment a bit at a loss of what to do.

Don't just stand there," John said, "go reapproach her."

"What? I didn't know we could reapproach."

"You weren't rejected by her, right? Your problem was simply one of logistics, never approach a woman walking head-on like that, at least not in a crowded place like this, because they're likely to pass you thinking you're just some weirdo in the crowd, like she just did. Do what you did last time, that was perfect, meaning to position yourself at her side, shoulders aligned, parallel, before you start talking."

"Somehow I feel reapproaching is weird, but okay, you're the Sensei, going to reapproach."

I ran a bit to catch up with her, and then slowed down as I got close to her, aligning my shoulders with hers, so we were side by side. I turned my head to face her, but she was looking straight ahead and hadn't noticed me, "Hey, I like those shades," I said.

She turned to look at me, "Don't have time, I'm late," she said, then looked forward again and bolted off running.

I stopped and turned around, and John was in front of me again.

"She's probably late for work or some meeting," John said, "she technically didn't reject you, she just had somewhere else to be. No biggie, just find the next one."

"Sensei," I said, "I noticed my anxiety went away during my last two approaches, I feel like I can approach anyone now, I think I'm cured."

"That's normal," John said, "you're not really cured. Basically, the first approach is like when you first get into a cold swimming pool, it seems terrifying at first, because the water's so cold, but once you're in the water you're body's already adjusted to it and you feel fine. If we take a break to eat, and then you start doing approaches again, the anxiety will come back, but it will lessen again after your first approach, that is until you stop making approaches, so I recommend you don't stop and go with it while you feel like this. So hurry and find the next one."

"Ah, that makes sense," I said, and immediately started looking around again.

"That one," I said, "the one with red hair and the blue jacket."

"Go for it!"

I quickly walked towards her and got myself into position, making sure our shoulders were aligned, "You're very beautiful," I said.

She turned to look at me looking upset, "Get away from me, creep!" she said, and then started to walk faster.

I stopped, wondering what had just happened.

"Looks like she rejected you," John said as he walked in front of me to face me.

"But why?"

"We'll never know, could be anything, but a word of advice, don't just tell a woman she's beautiful like that, never compliment her looks directly, stick with complimenting clothing instead, and don't ask me why right now, just find the next one."

"Yes Sensei."

I started looking around again, "Ponytail, red leather jacket," I said.

"You know what to do!"

I wasted no time getting myself in position by her side, turned my head towards her, "Cool jacket!" I said.

She looked at me, her eyes lit up and she smiled, "You're a bit direct, but sorry, I have a boyfriend," she said.

I made a sad face and quickly ejected, turning around and walking the other way.

John again appeared in front of me, "Thing is, when we approach random girls, we never know their current situation, they could be married, have a boyfriend, be late for work, etc. It's not necessarily you they are rejecting when they reject you, rather it's more about their current situation, although that doesn't mean that some women won't genuinely not like you and reject you for being you. You'll just naturally not click with some, but you'll click with others… Anyway, I guess what I'm saying is don't let rejections get you down, they will happen. Yes, every rejection kind of sucks, but they make you a better man, and having tons of rejections is well worth it to be able to have whatever successes you'll get. Furthermore, when a woman does reject you, she's actually doing you a favor, because you don't want to get involved with a woman who isn't in a place in her life where she is ready to be with a man like you. Rather than let it get you down, see every rejection as a teacher, and let it make you into a better man. Anyway, time to focus on the next one."

I must have done about sixty more approaches that day, taking just one 7-minute break for a short lunch which consisted of me and John buying hotdogs and eating them standing, and out of all of it, I only walked away with two phone numbers, all the rest either rejected me or were too busy to talk to me.

Two out of sixty is one out of thirty, which isn't that bad, I thought to myself.

To be able to have the phone numbers of a girl that I liked and who also liked me back was well worth being rejected by twenty-nine others. I would gladly be rejected twenty-nine times any day of the week to just have a chance with one woman that reciprocated my fondness for her.

"You did a lot today," John said, "and you got two numbers out of it, I'm proud of you. Let's go get dinner somewhere nice to celebrate, plan what you're going to do with those two numbers you have, and discuss what we're going to do tomorrow."

"Yes, Sensei!"

CHAPTER 6
DINNER

JOHN TOOK me to a steak house he raved about the whole way there, we sat at a booth, ordered our steaks, and then John started, "So let's talk, we need to drill deep into anything you're not sure about, so that we can nip it in the bud now, so you're ready for tomorrow."

"I understood that out of every thirty approaches, I'll meet one who's into me enough willing to give me her number, so that means if I ever feel lonely, all I have to do is thirty approaches and I'll meet someone, is that right? I'd be okay with just living life like that."

"Well, it doesn't always go like that, some days it might seem like one in thirty, some days it's nothing at all, and some days it might be like one in five. It all depends on a number of factors, most out of your control, and we can sum up all of those factors as being mostly luck, except one. The only one that you yourself actually control is skill, and the only way to improve skill is to do more approaches. It took me many years, Zeph, to get to the point where I'm at now as far as my skill. And while luck does still play a factor, your odds can be improved by perfecting the skill."

"I see John, well I have no other questions, I think I've got everything down, which is that after the first approach, my anxiety will lessen, and then I should do more approaches, get to know them, and ask for a number."

"Ahaha, well yeah, it certainly seems simple enough, but I assure you as you continue forward you'll be put in situations that will test you, and you'll realize that things are actually quite a bit more complicated than you once thought."

"So about the two numbers I did get, when should I be texting these women? And how quickly should I set up dates with them?"

"Ah yes, about them, show me the first one's number in your phone."

I pulled out my phone and showed John, "There," I said.

"Block and delete her now."

"What?!"

"And block and delete the other one too."

"Wait, but why? It took me a lot of effort to be able to get their numbers, and I really liked both of those women."

"Because you're still in training. I don't want you hooking up with any of the women you've met today. The purpose of this bootcamp is to improve your skills well enough so you can handle yourself in real life, not to meet your life partner during the bootcamp."

"No, I really liked those women, I may never see either of them again if I delete their contact information, they'll wonder what happened to me. I refuse, I can't delete them, I mean what if I was meant to marry one of them?"

"Marriage? Huh? You don't even really know them. And trust me, just because you have their numbers doesn't mean your first or second date will go well. The fact that you're already thinking about marriage just means I'm right in telling you to delete them from your phone."

"No, I can't, my ancestors won't let me."

"That's not your ancestors, that's the neediness inside you talking, we need to kill that neediness. You have to trust me,

Zeph, what I'm telling you to do is for your own good. I know you worked hard to get those numbers, but understand that this is just the beginning of your journey, if you want to really grow and become the type of man your ancestors would be proud of, you have to be willing to delete those numbers right now."

"And what if I don't."

"Don't question me, Zeph! I'm your Sensei, deleting them from your phone is not negotiable. I wanted you to number close today to show you it's not that difficult to do. But today was not about meeting your wife, today was about training you. You did well, and if you want to learn more of the magic you learned today you'll trust me and delete their numbers right now."

"But I can't."

"Look Zeph, every student who's ever been on this boot-camp deleted the numbers they got when I told them to, because they understood it was part of the training, some of them put up a tussle, the same as your doing now, but you didn't really meet those women today on your own. After the bootcamp, when you're on your own, and you ask for numbers, you can keep those."

"But why didn't you tell me that you wouldn't be letting me keep any numbers before you let me number close the women I met today?"

"Because then you wouldn't have tried so hard to number close anyone, but now it's time to delete them."

"Well, what about tomorrow, now that I know about this it's going to make me not try so hard tomorrow, won't it?"

"Not exactly, because tomorrow we'll be learning something entirely different."

"Please don't make me delete these numbers, Sensei, I'm begging you."

"The fact that you're begging me is all the more reason why you need to be deleting those numbers. Look, you have to know that you can't just rely on the fact that you have the number of a woman in your pocket. Your game needs to be tight enough that you can have nothing on your plate and still have a mentality of abundance. And that's exactly what we're going to be focusing on tomorrow, Abundance Mentality. Look, Zeph, you either block and delete the numbers out of your phone right now in front of me, or this bootcamp stops right here right now, and you'll never learn the real secrets you need to know that will carry you through the rest of your life."

"I hate you!" I said, as I blocked and deleted both numbers in front of John's eyes.

"Good," John said smiling, "proud of you again."

Just then our steaks arrived.

"So what will we do tomorrow, and what is this Abundance Mentality you speak of?" I said.

"Tomorrow, we're going to the local mall. It'll be similar to the train station. You know you can number close women, but this time I want you to not number close them, instead I want you to game so well that the women will be trying to number close you."

"Okay, um… And what was that thing about why I shouldn't compliment a woman's looks?"

"Well, it's just in my experience it doesn't work so well, it's something I learned very early on, because I used to try and compliment women on their looks and it always ended in rejection. Basically, they see a guy they don't know suddenly complimenting them on their looks as being too direct and it puts them off. I'm not saying you can't compliment a woman on her looks at all, just that it doesn't tend to work so well early on. It's a compliment better saved for after they get to know you a lot better, unless you've got massively good game skills. All the guidelines I'm sharing with you can be broken if you have massively good game skills, but it takes a lot of approaches to develop massively good game skills."

"Ah, I'd better write that down in my notes," I said as I noted it in my phone, "and what were you going to teach me about Abundance Mentality?"

"You'll learn about that tomorrow. After we finish our steaks, I'll drop you off, give you some time to process what happened today and get a good night's sleep, then tomorrow I'll pick you up at the same time, sound good?"

"Yes, I'll be ready at 7 am."

"Great!" John said as he bit into his steak.

"I'm really looking forward to tomorrow," I said, as I bit into my steak.

"That's a good sign, that you're looking forward to tomorrow. I think for the most part, you never really had anxiety. Once you do that first approach, you're fine. And anxiety on the first approach is totally normal for everyone. Mostly, all you ever needed to do in life was have someone show you that it's okay to approach and talk to women."

CHAPTER 7
ABUNDANCE MENTALITY

IT WAS 7 am and John was there on time.

"Morning," I said as I got into John's car.

"So, Zeph, today you're going to learn about Abundance Mentality."

"Yes, I've been wondering about that since you mentioned it last night, what exactly does Abundance Mentality mean?"

"Abundance Mentality is basically having the attitude that you have abundance, meaning that you're not going to feel bad if things don't go well with one woman, because you know that you can just find another woman if you need to. A lot of people have the mistaken notion that Abundance Mentality means having the contact information of lots of women that you've met, giving a sense of abundance. However, that can give us a false sense of Abundance Mentality, which is why I had you delete those women from your phone. You see, you don't want a false sense of Abundance Mentality, you need real Abundance Mentality, that means you need to be able to go anywhere knowing full well that you'll be able to meet a woman who's into you on the day if you needed to."

"And how exactly do I get real Abundance Mentality?"

"Well, it's like you said yesterday, you know that if you do 30 approaches, you'll most likely meet one woman who's also into you, so you just keep that in mind."

"That's it?" I said, "You made me delete two women that I worked so hard to number close yesterday just to learn that?" I said.

"Yup!" John answered as he parked the car in front of the mall. "And you need to prove today that you can maintain that same Abundance Mentality as you had with two women in your phone, even though you now have no women in your phone. Furthermore, today, you won't be number-closing any women, rather we're going to be focusing on making your game so tight that women are trying to number-close you. So you're not allowed to number close anyone, got it? The goal of today is to figure out how to make them number close you."

"But that's impossible. What you want of me is impossible."

"What happened to you yesterday, you previously thought was impossible, no? So we'll be doing more of that kind of magic."

"Well, how exactly do I get women to number close me?"

"Abundance Mentality."

"You keep saying, Abundance Mentality, but I feel like I don't really understand what it actually means."

"I know, but you'll soon not only understand those words, but you'll also get why I'm teaching the concept to you. In essence, Abundance Mentality is a kind of confidence, a kind of confidence that women can smell on you, and yesterday you didn't have it, but today you're going to develop it," John said as he opened the car door and we both started walking towards the mall."

For the rest of the walk to the mall which must have been about 5 minutes, we were both silent, as John led the way.

Approaching the entrance, there were a few people

smoking to the right and left of the entrance, John eyed them, and so did I, as he pushed the entrance doors open and I followed.

We walked down an empty hallway which brought us to the extremely crowded main strip of the mall which John turned left onto.

"Here we are," John said, "the mall. Already looks pretty crowded, huh? This place is full of women today, but it's still early, it'll get more crowded as the hours pass."

"Yeah, looks great!"

So, the first lesson is now. What I want you to do is to find a woman you like, just like we did yesterday, but before you talk to her, I want you to mentally imagine that you are a stud and that you can get any woman you want, but you can't just imagine it, you have to feel that you are that stud. You have to be that stud."

"And how exactly do I do that?"

"I told you, you have to imagine it, if you don't have an imagination it's going to be rough."

"I don't think I have an imagination."

"Look, the best boxers say that 90% of the fight is mental, and what we're doing is no different. We're playing a sport, a sport called 'Game,' and it's on you to mentally psyche yourself up. In the real world, after this bootcamp, I'm not going to be there to boost your confidence, you're going to have to do it yourself, just like a good athlete would. So this is practice time. And basically, if you approach any woman here and they smell the slightest bit of neediness on you, they will most likely reject you very quickly. So you need to imagine, as well as you can, that you are a man who is anything but needy, because you can go anywhere, a train station, a mall, or even just on a street and be able to start up a conversation with a woman, and leave together with the woman. And to do that, you need Abundance Mentality, which means a mentality where you feel like you are not attached to the outcome of getting a woman's number or bringing a woman somewhere with you. Meaning that if things go good it's nice, but if things don't go good, you're totally fine because you know that you'll find another one. Half the population of the world are women, and you're a man who has a very big advantage over other men, because you know how to approach them."

"I don't fully understand what you mean when you say I have an advantage."

"Oh come on Zeph, just yesterday you were approaching women in a train station and walked away with two numbers of women who wanted to meet you later. Remember that?"

"Yes, I remember."

"Have you ever met any man who's done that?"

"Done what?"

"Approach women they don't know in a train station and come out of it with two numbers."

"Actually, no, I haven't seen that anywhere."

"Exactly, and that's because most guys don't do that, they can't, because of fear. But you were able to cut through your fear and make your approaches."

"Whoa, now that I think about it, you're right, I've never seen anyone do what I did yesterday in my life, I do have an edge over other men knowing how to do that."

"Exactly, Zeph."

"Okay, I get your point… I like the one in the dirty blond hair wearing the pink jacket over there," I said as I motioned with my head.

"Now think abundance," John said, "think that you can have any woman you want, so you don't particularly need the interaction to go well. You're just going to go over and talk to her to find out more about her. Remember that you're outcome-independent, so it's not about the outcome. Though I'm not saying to not push for a desirable outcome, just that if it doesn't go that way, you're fine, maintain your composure, your coolness, your confidence, and always smile, even in the face of rejection. Got it?"

"Yes, I've got it, I'm going to approach."

"Good."

As I walked over to her, I could feel this fear in my gut that was telling me not to approach, it was my anxiety, it came back. I tried to ignore it, I focused on putting one foot on front of the other, and walked up on her side, and focused on making my shoulders parallel with hers, as John had taught me, in spite of feeling terrified. I couldn't think of an opening line for a moment, and then luckily one popped into my head. I turned my head to face her showing her a bright smile, "That jacket looks menacing, I like it," I said.

She looked at me, her beautiful blue eyes pierced through mine. "You're not my type," she said.

"What is your type?"

"I'm not sure, but not you."

I could feel those words hit hard, they were cold. I remembered what John said, thoughts entered my head that I could get any woman, I smiled at her, "Well, it was nice chatting with you," I said as I pulled a U-turn.

John appeared in front of me, "So why did you fail there?" John said.

"I'm not sure, she said I wasn't her type."

"Well, why do you think you failed?"

"I'm not sure, maybe I really just wasn't her type."

"It's possible, but I'll tell you what I think. I think your approach was a little weak. It's okay, it's your first approach of the day, I get it, and maybe you really just weren't her type, that's possible, but I think she sensed neediness in you and not abundance."

"I don't get it, Sensei, how can I show abundance?"

"Well, it's like you show interest in her, but without needing her to like you."

"And what can I say to show that?"

You see, Zeph, it's not what you say, it's what you're thinking. These women can actually read your mind. Whatever you think, they can see it written on your face. It's not enough to act outcome-independent, the thoughts in your head need to actually be outcome-independent. Meaning that you don't need the interaction to go well because you are a man with a very big advantage over other men, and so you have lots of options, and your thoughts need to reflect that. Keep that in mind, and let's try again."

"Yes Sensei," I said.

Then I looked around. "Brown hair, black sweater, green jeans," I said to John, and then started walking towards her.

I approached and made my shoulders parallel with hers, hoping that this one would appreciate my effort, and then looked at her, "I like the color of your jeans."

She didn't turn her head, didn't react, didn't even notice me. Again I said, "I like the color of your jeans," but still she ignored me. I wasn't sure what else to say, so I made a U-turn again, and there was John.

"I see you blew out again. What happened? What could you have done better?"

"She just ignored me, I don't know what I could have done better."

"Well, it's obvious she just ignored you, I saw that. But you ejected a little early, I would have tried to hang in there just a little longer."

"But I didn't know what to say."

"Not knowing what to say and maintaining a positive vibe, even in the midst of awkward silence, is not necessarily a bad thing, I mean it wouldn't bother a man with an Abundance Mentality. Try to stick in a little longer on the next one."

I felt like John wasn't fully understanding my frustrations, but all I could say was, "Yes Sensei."

"You're doing good," John said, "just need to get into a groove, I know you feel like I don't understand your frustrations, I do. I've felt exactly what you're feeling right now many a time. Don't worry though, these things tend to self-correct if you keep making approaches."

I felt upset at myself, but John was right, I should keep making approaches, and so looked around again. "Black straight hair, fuzzy purple jacket," I said to John, and started walking towards another woman.

I did the same thing as before and made my shoulders parallel with hers, turned my head towards her, "I've never seen a jacket like that before, it really stands out, what's it made of?" I said.

"Oh," she said turning towards me, "it's synthetic fur, nothing special, but, yes, it does tend to stand out."

"Can I touch it I said?"

"Of course, you can," she said laughing.

"Doing good Zeph," I could hear John whisper at me from behind.

"That feels really nice," I said as I felt her sleeve.

"That's why I bought it," she said, "I just really liked how it felt."

"Hi, I'm John, nice to meet you," I said, staring directly into her eyes as I put out my hand.

"Stop walking," I heard John whisper-scream at me from behind.

So I stopped, and she stopped.

"That's good, she stopped when you stopped, that means you have compliance, it means she likes you!" I heard John whisper-screaming at me as he let out a soft laugh.

"I'm Jessica," she said, putting out her hand to grab mine.

As we held hands looking into each other's eyes, there was an awkward silence for maybe like a full 10 seconds. I wasn't sure what to say. Then it came to me, "My mind hasn't started working yet this morning for some reason, wanna grab a coffee?"

"I would," she said smiling. I couldn't believe how fast this was happening.

"That's the magic! Amazing!" I could hear John whisper-scream, even louder than last time.

"Is that your friend whisper-screaming to you?" Jessica said.

"Ah, yeah, that's my friend, don't worry about it, he has something to do," I said holding her hand in mine and looking around for a cafe to go to. I spotted one, and started walking with her towards it.

During the coffee, we must have talked for about 30 minutes, I learned she was a freelance web designer, liked to work out, and was in her last year of college studying IT. Our conversation ended with her saying, "I don't want to steal you away from your friend since you came here together, and I've got to get to another cafe actually to study with one of my friends."

We both finished our lattes, and as we exited the cafe she handed me her phone with her profile page showing her number on the screen.

I put her number in my phone and then texted her a smiley face.

"I'll call you," I said, and then we both parted ways.

That was pretty good, John said, "She asked for your number, huh?"

"Yes, she did."

One out of three asked for your number so far, let's see if you can maintain that ratio for the rest of the day.

I did about 20 more approaches, all rejections. Then me and John had Chinese noodles for lunch in the food court, then I did about 40 or so more approaches, and towards the end of that I took another woman to the same cafe for a coffee, and that woman also asked for my number and we parted ways in much the same way.

As we left the mall, John said, "I think you have Abundance Mentality down. Really excellent that 2 women actually asked for your number, most guys couldn't pull that off, you did real good today!"

"Thanks, Sensei, I really appreciate the kind words," I said. It felt so good hearing that from John. I was in total awe of this new world that John had opened up for me, a world of me being able to meet new women practically anywhere. If I could replicate anywhere near what I did at the train station or at the mall today I was sure to never have women problems again.

"Come on, Zeph, let's go grab some dinner and wrap up this bootcamp."

I felt sad at the thought that this was all coming to a close. It meant that I would be on my own from now on without John there having my back, but I'll never forget what John did for me. This was truly life-changing, it was well worth the 4K I'd spent to learn from John I thought, as I never would have figured all this stuff out on my own.

CHAPTER 8
THE SECOND DINNER

JOHN TOOK me to the same steakhouse he took me to yesterday, we sat across from each other in a booth and ordered our meals.

"Okay, so you've been through this bootcamp, learned how to approach women, figured out that it's not all about talking or even what you say, and got 2 more numbers today, I'm proud of you, but now you're on your own. Oh, one more thing, I would like to ask that you write me a testimonial through the form on my website."

"Wait, what? That's it? You're just going to end it like that?"

"Well, yes and no. If you have any questions about anything, you can feel free to ask them over the course of this last meal together."

"Of course, I have questions. I mean up until two days ago, I hadn't been on a date with a woman at all, I mean not ever, not ever in my life. And suddenly I'm meeting all these women and getting phone numbers, you can't just leave me hanging here. I suddenly feel so, so sad. I'm going to miss you."

"You'll get over it the moment you get some women in

your life. I'm confident you know what to do from here. You just do like we did today and yesterday, and don't drink anymore, and I know you'll be fine."

"Wait Sensei, what if I have questions? You don't have any after-bootcamp support or something? Or couldn't we hang out together sometime?"

Look, "Zeph, I'm flattered that you think so highly of me, I really am, but you're going to have to take the reigns from here, just remember what we discussed, about your ancestors, and especially about Abundance Mentality, because I didn't feel that you have that completely down yet, though I think you understood the concept enough that you'll figure it out as you perfect your skills out there in the field, meeting women. I'd actually never thought of offering an after-bootcamp support service, but I'll give some serious thought to it, if I should offer such a service. But if I don't, this will be our last meeting together."

"Sensei, no, you can't just leave me like this? I look up to you, I need you in my life, I don't want to end what we've got here."

"Look, Zeph, I've held up my part of the bootcamp deal, I trained you, and I'm confident you'll be okay from here on out. There are many others like you who need my help now, other men with women problems. You know all you need to know now to have many many amazing and spectacular relationships with women. What else do you want from me?"

"Well, what if a woman gives me an issue, like what if it starts out great and then the relationship goes bad?"

"I don't do relationships Zeph, I just do the part of how to meet women. As far as relationships go, that's a whole different ball of wax. Though there is one thing I can tell you, and that is if a woman ever gives you too much stress where you feel absolutely terrible, end the relationship as quickly as possible, but don't end it in a harsh way, show respect to her as you end it, and then block her on everything so there is no way for her to contact you, and never see her again. I mean, hopefully, none of your relationships get to that point, but if they do, then that's what you have to do."

"That makes sense. Thanks for the great advice, and thanks for all you've done for me. I just kind of feel like you're kind of like the father that I always needed that I never had. I'm really going to miss you," I said as tears started to roll down my cheeks.

"What? You're going to start crying, don't do that, get yourself together man."

I suddenly burst into tears, and grabbed a napkin to dry and hide my sad face, "I'm really going to miss you, Sensei. It feels like the girls didn't even matter so much as compared with all you've done for me."

"I can't refuse a grown man who cries. Tell you what, Zeph, I'll make you a one-time offer. If you throw me an extra grand right now, I'll offer you three emergency support calls, meaning if you ever find yourself in some kind of situation related to women and not sure what to do, you can call me. However, you shouldn't be calling me every day, it's just for an emergency, so you need to try to figure out how to resolve whatever the issue is yourself, and if what you're doing isn't working, then give me a call. How does that sound?"

Three emergency calls with John? Yes! My eyes lit up and I started to smile as I dried my face further with the napkin. "I gladly thank you for the offer, Sensei, um… I don't have cash on me right now, could we stop at an ATM."

"Sure Zeph."

"I appreciate it, Sensei."

"Oh, and one more thing, Zeph, before I forget, this is actually the most important pickup artist secret you'll ever hear."

"What? Another secret? What is it?"

"Zeph, this is not just another secret, it is The Secret. You need to promise never to reveal this to anyone, okay?"

"Of course, Sensei."

"Okay, so this is the real secret I'm going to tell you now, the real secret that men in the know will keep from other men for the entire history of the human race. Now, before I tell it to you, promise me you'll never tell another soul, okay?"

CHAPTER 9
WHY I WROTE THIS BOOK

IT'S BEEN three years since I last saw John that night, and I haven't yet had a need to use any of my three emergency calls, and I've approached thousands upon thousands of women since then, and I'm currently engaged now.

Some might think I'm a fool for paying John so much money for the bootcamp and for emergency phone calls that I never used, and perhaps I was, but there was no one else to guide me at that time, and you have to understand I was at my wit's end and in a very bad mental state, and John helped me to get out of that.

That said, I've learned his secrets, and I've field-tested them on the front lines, approaching hordes of women, and after all of that, I've come away with some realizations, which I'd like to share with you in the next chapter, and then The Big Secret which I'll reveal to you in the chapter after that one. However, before we delve into all of that, I'd like to, first of all, share with you in this chapter why I've chosen to reveal what I'm about to reveal to you in this book.

You see, my experience with John was my first step into this pickup world. And after my bootcamp with him, I realized there are tons more pickup artist gurus out there teaching men from all walks of life even more pickup artist secrets, with each guru claiming that their strategies and techniques are the best, that they know some big secret that all the other pickup artist gurus aren't teaching.

What this pickup artist thing really is, is it's an industry, an industry that maintains the guise of being a community, but is actually all about making a profit from desperate men. Now, I'm not saying what pickup artist gurus are teaching doesn't work. I mean, what John taught me sure did work for me. But what I'm saying is that the vast majority of men don't actually need to pay a guru to figure out how to meet and do well with women, they just need to understand a few basic principles, and if they understand those few basic principles, that's all they really need to know, and I'll soon break those down for you.

The reason I wrote this book was not to put down pickup artists or pickup artist gurus, and not to put down any dating gurus. I mean, I get that pickup artist gurus are just one segment of an even bigger for-profit industry that makes even more than the pickup artist gurus, and that would be the dating industry, which consists of dating apps, expensive colognes, and all manner of gimmicks that make various claims that they can help men to attract the opposite sex. And I'm fine with all of those companies and organizations existing. They exist for a reason, and that reason is that there is a market out there of desperate men in need, men who don't know how to go about getting a woman, men who broke up with their girlfriend or got divorced and now find themselves back at square one, men who are simply introverts for whatever reason, and so on. So of course companies and gurus will pop up, seeing a demand in the market, a demand created by all kinds of men hoping to be saved, to be saved from how hard modern society makes things on them.

Anyway, the reason I wrote this book is simply to help other men that are like the man I used to be, to explain to other men that they don't need to buy any products from a company or hire a pickup artist guru, dating coach, or anyone else to help them to be able to do well with women, because if I had to do it all over again, I would have done it differently. That might seem easy for me to say, since I'm now engaged to be married in eight months, but I'm talking to the man I was before I approached thousands of women, the unhappy man who was desperate to give anything a go if it would help me to simply be able to have a normal and successful relationship with a woman that I find attractive.

So taking the secrets that I've learned, I'm going to explain to you what I would have explained to me before I had ever taken John's bootcamp. Essentially, I'm going to reveal to you the secrets that I stole from John.

CHAPTER 10
REALIZATIONS

SO BEFORE I get into The Big Secret, which I'll reveal in the next chapter, I'd like to first of all share with you the realizations I've had over my time after my bootcamp where I pushed myself to approach women daily.

Realization 1:

My first realization is what Abundance Mentality actually is. I never really understood what it was when John tried to explain it to me, and I actually think the words Abundance Mentality are poor words to describe the concept. Basically, it's more like a self-fulfilling prophecy based upon the assumptions that we draw prior to approaching a woman. If we approach a woman holding the assumption in our head that it's pointless, or that it won't work out, or if we think something like, 'How can such a beautiful woman ever be interested in a guy like me?' Or if we have any doubts in the back of our mind regarding our looks, our personality or about anything about us that we recognize as a weakness, those thoughts lingering in the back of our mind are highly likely, without our conscious intent, to have an influence over our interaction. This does not only apply to talking to women, but to a variety of aspects in our life. For example, let's say we go to a job interview for what we perceive to be a high-level job, but deep inside we feel like we are less than enough to obtain a job like that. That feeling of feeling less than enough will translate into us acting in a way during the job interview that will likely cause us to not get the job, because the interviewer might see us as desperate or weak.

So basically, Abundance Mentality is a kind of mental state powered by our ego where we are not doubting ourselves in the back of our mind. So essentially every time we approach a woman, we need to feel like we are good enough as we are, good enough for the woman we're talking to, to accept us. And we'll never obtain that natural Abundance Mentality through any other way other than through the experience of approaching and talking with many many women. John wanted me to delete the women in my phone, because having women in your phone gives a kind of artificial Abundance Mentality. Basically, it's like if you have a job already, and you're interviewing for other jobs, you know that if you fail any of those interviews you are safe, because you have a job already, so when you interview, you'll naturally present yourself differently to a company knowing that you're fine to fail the interview because you don't actually need this new job. However, if you didn't have a job for a while and have bills to pay, you're more desperate to get a job, and if you're not good at hiding that sense of desperation within you it will likely show and could affect your chances of getting the job. Though, if you know you're a master of the art of whatever job you are interviewing for, whether you're truly desperate to get a job or not, the fact that you know, you know that the job you're interviewing for would be a piece of cake for you is basically a very real kind of Abundance Mentality. But if you have doubts in your head, it will affect things, unless the company you're interviewing with is desperate to hire.

So essentially Abundance Mentality is simply being able to talk to a woman, or go to a job interview, or do anything else in life where you know someone will judge you, and do it without having any doubts in your head. Some people can eliminate their doubts with little effort, but other people might not be able to do so without having more experience under their belt.

While Abundance Mentality does give you a better chance at being successful, it doesn't mean that without Abundance Mentality you can't still be successful. So I would say it's not a defining factor for having success with women or with anything else, but it does put the odds in your favor enough that having an Abundance Mentality will aid you more times than not. However, it's not something we really need to consciously think about, because it will come naturally through repetition of doing approaches or doing job interviews, or doing whatever. But if by thinking about it we are able to consciously eliminate our doubts about ourself, and we actually happened to have little experience, then eliminating our doubts would help greatly. However, Abundance Mentality is still not as powerful as real-world, authentic experience.

I mean, I get the lesson John was trying to teach me about it, but I don't think it was worth having to delete the two women out of my phone.

And in short, my realization is that ultimately Abundance Mentality doesn't matter so much as actual experience doing something matters, because when we have a lot of experience doing something, and we have a very strong sense of confidence that we can do it with our eyes closed and know exactly how things will play out, that sense of confidence that only experience can give us trumps any kind of mentality that exists, including Abundance Mentality.

Realization 2:

Many approaches won't go as we expect. We as men assume that a woman will reject us because she is out of our league, and while many times that may be true, it has happened to me enough times that approaches have not gone the way I expected. Meaning that a woman who I was near certain would reject me because she clearly seemed to be out of my league did not reject me. I think this is the hardest thing for men to believe, as we all kind of assume that our expectations of what will happen to us when we approach and talk to a woman is what will happen. But based on what I've seen, I'd say you need to throw all your expectations out the window. Because all of my expectations were proven wrong more times than not.

This realization helped me to create a new model about what to expect that I feel is more accurate than my previous one, but even with a better model in my head, the unexpected will still happen. The point is, it's always worth trying to approach a woman, because sometimes when you're sure you'll be rejected, you may just be surprised at what happens.

Realization 3:

I never needed a bootcamp, because there are no actual secrets to doing well with women except one secret thing, and I'll get into that one secret thing in the next chapter. I mean, yes there are things we can do that would increase our chances of doing well with women and seeing faster results. But over the long-term, knowing those things isn't really going to help us so much as opposed to just knowing one secret thing. And I'm going to just reveal it to you now to make sense of everything. On to the next Chapter!

CHAPTER 11
THE BIG SECRET

JOHN TOLD me before that maintaining a positive attitude, an open mind, and the motivation to keep trying is really the whole secret, and he wasn't necessarily wrong about that, yes those things are important to maintain, but that's not The Big Secret that I'm referring to.

Okay, now for the big reveal, the one thing you need to know to give you all kinds of dating options, and why you don't need to actually pay someone to teach you about women. Because if you just know this one thing, and if you do it over and over again, and if you make an effort to learn from your mistakes and get better at it, then every other thing, your bad habits and your mistakes, will all auto-correct by virtue of doing just this one thing.

And I should, first of all, say that most people don't want to hear this one, because it's hard, it takes a ton of courage, and it will take you way out of your comfort zone if you're not used to doing it. Now before I mention it, I should say that some of you might see this as multiple things, and say, "Aha, you're telling us multiple things, so it's really not just one thing!"

And my counter to that is, "The multiple things I'm telling you are all part of that one thing."

And this one thing is what all guys who seem naturally good with women who would never pay for a bootcamp or read a book like this are already doing, and it's the one thing that all pickup artist gurus will tell you that you need to do, whether you take a bootcamp with a pickup artist or whether you read a book written by a pickup artist.

And anyway, in a nutshell, the only thing you need to do is whenever you see a woman you like you approach her. That's it, that's all you need to do. That is the one big secret to being successful with women, is to simply have the courage to quickly talk to a woman you think you like the moment you see her. I say, 'You think you like,' because after you talk to her you might change your mind and decide you don't like her, but you never really know if you'll still like her or not if you don't talk to her in the first place.

You see, any guy who seems naturally good with women, who some call a natural, simply figured this thing out early on, that approaching and talking to women is the whole secret to the game.

And with me paying thousands for lessons through a bootcamp with a so-called pickup artist master, the main activity I was being pushed to do in that bootcamp was approach women. Yes, John gave pointers along the way, but none of those pointers were actually needed I soon found out through doing approaches on my own.

In fact, had I never took a bootcamp and someone told me that I need to change my act, and that I need to start approaching women and talking to women in real life, and in spite of rejections just keep approaching and talking to women, I'm 100% sure I would have gotten the same results.

None of John's advice was necessarily wrong, I do honestly believe he gave me advice because he cared about my best interests, but I do in a way believe he scammed me, and I fell for the scam, because I believed it, I believed that my success was due to the secrets he was teaching me. But the only real secret was that all I needed to do was to get into a habit of approaching and talking to women I don't know, and some would like me and some wouldn't like me, and that would be that. And that's the reality of things.

Yes, there is a whole dating industry built around selling men secrets, secrets to be successful with women, when the truth of the matter is that all one needs to be successful with women is right under their nose, but they can't see it. There is a fantasy that for each thing we want, there is some secret we need to learn, and if we just learn that secret, then it will fix all of our problems in that area.

I can't tell you how many times I've seen a program suggesting that you can learn a language in a day or in a week, and the truth is you can't learn a language in a day or in a week. But many people choose to spend their time searching for secrets on how to learn a language faster than just doing the hard work of studying the grammar and memorizing words and phrases in the language they want to learn.

And what I'm telling you is that there really are no secrets for getting good with women. And getting good with women is all about approaching and talking to women you don't know, since talking to women you don't know increases the number of women you do know, which increases your odds of finding a woman who's into you.

The truth of the matter is that while you can choose who you approach, it is the woman who chooses you, meaning it's the woman's choice as to whether she likes you enough to want to see you again. But a woman can't have the option of choosing you in the first place unless you give her a sample of your personality by putting yourself out there which can only be done by approaching women.

Mathematically, let's imagine that there are an infinite

number of women out there, and that every day you could talk to maybe thirty (if you didn't have to work), since it takes time to talk to each one. Eventually, after talking to many you would meet one who would be very interested in you.

Well, I've got good news for you, there are already enough women on Earth that you could talk to thirty a day for the rest of your life and you wouldn't have met them all, so there are essentially an infinite number of women out there for you. The thing is, if you work a job or run your own business, or go to school, you probably don't have the time to talk to so many women each day, but you could probably talk to one a day, or maybe you could talk to five a day, this all depends on how much time you have.

The point is, all you need to do is to take some time out of your day to attempt to talk to some new women every day, whether that be at a mall, at a train station, or wherever it may be, the same way you saw me trying to talk to women in this book. Yes, without paying someone for a bootcamp you won't have a person like John there to guide you. Yes, it will take an enormous amount of courage on your behalf to approach and start up that first conversation with a woman you don't know, but all following approaches and conversations on the day should prove to be easier, and by making it a habit to do this daily, you are putting the mathematical odds in your favor that you will meet women who like you who you also like. And that is the whole big secret of pickup artistry and game.

So that is the one thing you need to do and keep doing. The multiple things that I was referring to at the beginning of this chapter that you also need to do are basically just common sense things, like be sure to hold eye contact with any woman you're talking to, be sure to know what you're going to say to her upon making your approach, like compliment an article of clothing she's wearing, and if the conversation goes well then be sure to ask for her number. It takes a lot of courage to ask for a number, because there is a chance that she may refuse and you'll feel rejected, but just ask for the number anyway because you'll be kicking yourself later if you don't. And that's all you really need to know. And if someone just told me that was all I would have needed to do many years ago, I would have never needed John, I would have never had woman problems in the first place and I probably would have already been engaged to someone.

So you see, my problem was that I had chosen a path of inaction, because I didn't even know there was a path of action I could have been taking. Don't be like me and let your life slip by without ever approaching and talking to any women, rather you want to be approaching and talking to women as much as possible with whatever free time you have.

If you simply do what I'm saying here, yes you'll get rejected a lot at first, and it will hurt, but as you keep going you'll get successes, and those successes will be evidence that what you're doing is working, which should motivate you even more to make more approaches.

I repeat, there are no secrets to getting women, the fact that you think there are secrets is all in your head. Thousands of years ago humans didn't have advanced technology or a highly advanced society, the men back then knew instinctively that if they saw a woman they like they should go and talk to her, because they could be eaten by a sabertooth tiger tomorrow, so the chance may never come again. But in the modern day and age, we've lost our way, so it's not so apparent for most men to simply go up to and talk to women.

Do you think women dress nice and put on makeup because they don't want men to talk to them? It's very flattering for any woman for a man to attempt to start a conversation with her. And that's the whole reason women dress nice and put on makeup for the most part, so they can be attractive, and being attractive is all about attracting others to come up and talk to you.

And all these pickup artist gurus really teach you to do is to approach, yes they tell you a bunch of other stuff, but to just make approaches is the main thing they teach, and all the other stuff is just fluff for the most part.

Also, the more approaches you make, the more experience you get at doing approaches, which means your approaches will get better and better over time through experience, which will make you seem even more attractive to women. Yes, women do notice a difference in a man who's never made an approach compared to a man who's made over a hundred approaches compared to a man who's made over a thousand approaches.

And I don't care what age you are, whether you're in your twenties, thirties, forties or fifties, etc. It's never too late to start getting approaches under your belt.

The title of this book, "Secrets I Stole from a Pickup Artist," refers to the fact that all the secrets are simply the simple act of approaching and talking to women regularly and everything that goes along with that. If you simply just approach and try to talk to every woman that catches your eye and continue to do that and not give up on it, and see all rejections you get as constructive feedback, you'll be able to meet all kinds of nice women you would have never even known had existed before, and you'll eventually get a girl-friend, and possibly even get engaged, like me, and become a very happy man.

If you don't listen to what I've said, sure you can tell your-self my advice was all bunk and go on through life looking for the secrets to attracting women. However, what you'll find if you keep searching is exactly what I've already told you. You won't find anything new, there are no other secrets to learn, because everything you'll find will all lead back to one thing, which is approaching and talking to women. We can debate whether approaching is one thing, and talking to women is another thing, is it just one secret or is it two secrets, and perhaps making eye contact is another thing, and perhaps asking for a phone number is another thing, but I simply call it The Big Secret, because if you just make an approach, of course you're going to talk to the woman you approach, and of course if you're talking to someone you're going to make eye contact with them, and of course if you like the person you're talking to and if it's obvious they also like you then, of course, you're going to have to ask for her number, right? So all these little actions are actually one big action, one big secret, which we can just call Approaching Women. Everything else that anyone says is BS.

How did your dad meet your mom, well if you ask him, probably he approached her, or maybe they were in a class together, but even in that case he had to at some point talk to her and ask her out on a date which is basically the same as approaching and talking, or maybe your mom approached him. In any case, someone approached, and someone talked, and that's the case for every relationship on Earth, except for maybe people whose parents stick them in an arranged marriage. So I think you get what I'm saying here, that the main thing you need to focus on to get good with women is to get good at the process of approaching women, and to understand, mathematically speaking, that the more approaches we do the better the odds increase that we'll meet women that we really like who also really like us back.

It's really that simple. But of course, there is a whole dating industry out there that wants you to think it's not that simple, that wants to sell you courses, bootcamps, dating strategy seminars and whatnot. And what I'm really saying here is that you don't need any of that stuff if you just focus on the one Big Secret that I've just made clear to you.

Whether you believe me or not, it's your prerogative. I get some guys will think, 'I really don't look so handsome, I've got problems, why would a woman ever be into me?' And all I can say, is that you'd be surprised at what kinds of women would overlook your flaws and be into you, if you'd only just make an attempt regularly to put yourself out there and talk to women. As I've said, it's the women who chooses you, but you can't be chosen if you're not even putting yourself out there at all. Like do you really think a woman is going to approach you? I mean, it can happen, and it actually has happened to me before, but in my experience, it's kind of a rare thing to be approached by a woman, so why wait for a chance that may never come? Instead, just make a decision today to take the initiative to approach, and put the odds in your favor.

Even if you think you're not so handsome, just having the courage to approach a woman and talk to her tells her that you're a man with confidence, because most men in this day and age do not have the courage to approach a woman and talk to her, and there is simply nothing more attractive to most women than a confident man. I know this, because that's what women have told me, I've had conversations with women about this very topic, and they see men who have the courage to start up a conversation with them as being confident, and as such being attractive, even if the man doesn't have the body or face of a model.

So put your insecurities aside, and listen to someone who's telling you for your own good what you need to do to fix your perhaps currently nonexistent love life. You need to find the courage to approach and talk to women, and you need to start doing that as soon as possible, like how about today? Or does the thought of approaching and talking to a woman today scare you? If it scares you, then the only way to overcome that fear is by taking action and trying to make an approach today in spite of your fear.

And don't approach a woman being all rude to her. Be

kind, courteous, show respect, and if she rejects you then leave her alone and find another woman to approach.

You need to be able to motivate yourself to approach and talk to women is what it all comes down to. If you can't do that, it's clear why you are not successful with women. If you can do that, then success will come, but you shouldn't give up at the sign of the first rejection, you have to keep doing it with the knowledge that you'll have to take a lot of rejections before you finally meet a woman who's into you.

Also, with each approach, if things don't go so well, you need to think about what went wrong, and what you could be doing better, and you need to make adjustments so that you can make better approaches. What kind of adjustments you make will be different for each person. Like, if women who you approach keep telling you that you smell, then it's kind of obvious you need to shower or use deodorant to fix that problem. If women you approach keep telling you that they don't like something you said, then it's obvious don't say that thing again, change what you say to something nicer. These are all just common sense things that you'll figure out if you make the effort to keep approaching women.

Another thing you could do, is if you keep getting rejected and you don't know why, you could just ask each new woman who rejects you why they rejected you, and what it was about your approach that caused her to reject you. If she gives you a reason and it seems like an honest one, then maybe that's something you need to consider changing about your style of approaching women.

CHAPTER 12
DEFINING APPROACH ANXIETY

NOW THAT I'VE revealed The Big Secret, I believe that is enough for most guys to do well with women. Though if you know The Big Secret, and if you still don't feel like you can do well with women, then more than likely you have a confidence problem.

Confidence is a tricky thing, but in the best interest of giving more to my readers than simply my bootcamp experience with a pickup artist guru and what I took away from it, and since now I believe that everything that pickup artists teach is BS with the exception of telling their students to approach women, I'd like to dig deeper into the area of confidence, because this is an area I know all too well. Because as you've seen in this book, I had major confidence issues. So if you have a similar issue to the one I had, then what we're going to talk about next will likely be of great importance to you, because what we're going to get into next is to focus on what we need to do to fix the only obstacle in your path which would be your confidence issue, which we can also call approach anxiety.

I'd like to, first of all, say that it's possible that you have some other kind of anxiety that is a medical condition, and in that case, I would refer you to talking to a doctor or other such medical professional, because this book does not offer any medical or psychological advice or any cure to any such problem. What I am offering is simply the techniques I used to fix my approach anxiety as general advice for those who don't have any true medical issues but find that they get anxious when trying to approach and talk to women who they like.

In this book, you've already seen, through my story, some of the things that I initially did to help me overcome my very strong approach anxiety, but you didn't see after John was out of my life how I had to overcome once again the strong approach anxiety that was trying to stop me from talking to women, and what I had to do to overcome my approach anxiety once and for all. Despite what John told me, I found out that it is possible to fix approach anxiety once and for all, but before we get to that part we need to first of all define what approach anxiety actually is.

At its core, approach anxiety is a fear like any other fear, some people have a fear of heights, some people have a fear of snakes, some people have a fear of spiders, some people have a fear of public speaking, and some people have a fear of approaching women. While a fear of heights, snakes, or spiders makes logical sense because it's a fear that protects us from death, a fear of public speaking or a fear of approaching doesn't make logical sense because it doesn't protect us from anything, so what we are really trying to do is overcome a fear that doesn't make logical sense.

A very common story pickup artists like to tell is that approach anxiety is something that all men have hardwired in their brains from times when humans lived in tribes, and there were a limited number of women in our tribe, and so one rejection by one woman one time could mean failure to be able to reproduce, or if we approached the wrong woman it could mean death. And while it's a very nice story, there is no scientific proof that this is where approach anxiety actually comes from, although it is a good theory.

Anyway, we already know what we need to do in order to get better with women, but without taking the fear factor out of the equation, we are not likely to do it. So we now need to focus on just that, how to take the fear factor out of the equation.

CHAPTER 13
THE 3 THINGS THAT KILL APPROACH ANXIETY

THERE ARE three main things that are sure to kill approach anxiety that we must be willing to adopt.

The first is motivation, and not just our motivation, but the source of our motivation. Because truth be told, if we can understand on a deep level what motivates us, and the source of what motivates us, and if we take it seriously, any kind of fears we have will mostly be gone.

The second is a sense of urgency, which means an understanding of the passage of time and the eventuality of death. We need to realize that death can happen and does happen, and that our life on this Earth is very short. And if we can wrap our heads around that, we can actually undo all fears about anything.

And the third is seeing approach anxiety for what it really is, which I'll soon explain in greater detail.

And these three components are, in a nutshell, what we need to delve very deeply into. And if you're willing to hear what I have to say about these three things, and if you keep an open mind as I tell you what I know about them, I'm very sure they'll kill your approach anxiety forever, and you'll never have it again.

When I say you'll never have it again, I really mean that. This book will cure your approach anxiety completely, and if for some reason it doesn't it simply means that you haven't really integrated or fully understood what I've told you on one of the three things, and you'll need to reread this book, or at least the chapter about the part that you haven't integrated so well into your thought process.

CHAPTER 14
MOTIVATION

SO NOW WE'LL get into the first component we need to master, and that is motivation. While many of you simply think the source of your motivation for wanting to get good with women is to get a girlfriend, or have girlfriends, or have a life partner, just that alone won't do it, and that alone is a very weak kind of motivation. But don't feel bad if one of those has been the source of your motivation all this time, it's not that the source of motivation was wrong, rather the problem is that your source of motivation was lacking other components to strengthen its effectiveness at motivating you to take action in spite of fear, in spite of a life or death situation. We're not talking about a real-life or death situation, but since the act of approaching for those of us with approach anxiety feels like a life-or-death situation, we have to treat it like that.

So what we need are ways to strengthen our motivation, and we can't strengthen it with something fake, we must strengthen it with something real, because anything fake will feel fake, and so the way we strengthen it has to feel real, and for it to feel real, it has to be real, and the good news is that what I'm about to tell you that will strengthen your motivation not only will feel real, it is real!

Not only does our motivation have to be real, but our motivation has to be tied to a higher purpose that has a consequence should we fail to live up to our higher purpose, and it has to have a good story behind it. Just look at any soldier who has ever proudly went to war willing to face death for some higher purpose, that is exactly the kind of higher purpose we need to have embedded in our brain to fuel our motivation when it comes to something like making approaches.

So where does a higher purpose come from? Well, silly as it sounds it comes from a story, not a fiction story, but a story we believe to be true, so we have to buy into our own story. And you are free to make your own story, but what I'm going to do is to share with you the story that got me through, and I hope my motivational story will become your story, but if you don't like mine, feel free to create your own similar story to tell yourself. Anyway, this is my story:

So my motivation was always that I wanted a girlfriend, but giving it a higher purpose, my story is that I am ordained by my ancestors and the highest power in the universe to find my partner in life so that I can have many children who in turn have many children, and thus spread my descendants and their descendants throughout the world and eventually throughout the universe, and if I fail to do that, the consequences are the death and destruction of my bloodline, which translates into my life being a failed one, so I can't let that happen. Failure is not an option for me, for if I fail, I fail not just myself but I also fail my ancestors as well as the highest power in the universe. And after death, I'd have to face them, and I don't want to face them telling them I failed them. And so, I must live up to my purpose, I must live up to my destiny, I must live up to what I was ordained to do, and so I cannot fail. Failure would mean the end of my existence and would cause great damage to the forces who put me here as a conscious force in this human body. Not only that, but me failing would damage all good in the universe and would strengthen the forces of evil, the ones who don't want me to succeed. I can't let the dark forces win, to do so is to not just fail myself, my ancestors, and the highest power, but to also fail every-thing that is good in the universe, and so my insignificant fear means nothing because failure is not even an option. Thus, I must approach, I must approach for all that is good and wholesome and for everything I and my ancestors stand for, I must approach to gain the favor of the highest power in the universe and to keep the power strong of all that is good in the universe, because if I don't approach, evil will win and gain the upper hand, and the universe will turn into a vile wretched place with no more blue skies, no more pizza, no more cotton candy, no more women, and no more of anything much that would make life worth living. So by the power of all the forces that I represent, I must see this thing through and immediately approach every woman I see until I achieve my goal, my purpose, my destiny. That is the source of my motivation to approach.

And when you have a motivational story for yourself like that, it should be all you need.

CHAPTER 15
SENSE OF URGENCY

OKAY, this is going to get grim, but with a silver lining, so hold on to your shades, because we need to discuss the prospect of death.

You see, back in the day when our ancestors existed on the Earth, death was a very real possibility. You could be killed by anything, you could be killed by a virus, an animal, an insect, or even by another person or group of people, or you could even starve to death if you were unable to find food. Society back then was not like the friendly society we live in today with police a phone call away and bouncers or security personnel making sure no fights happen in every venue where large numbers of people gather. Some might argue that society is not so friendly with all of the bad things on the news, but if we compare today to way back in the day, things are definitely a heck of a lot safer. Aside from a lower chance of being attacked by another human, you also have an extremely low chance of getting killed by an animal or insect, and there are all sorts of medicines today to help you recover from diseases that would have previously wiped you and your whole family out, and finally there is absolutely no way that you're going to starve to death, like even if you were to try to steal food and you were caught, you'd go to prison where they'd give you free food every day.

It's good in one sense that life is far safer today than it ever previously was for humans, but in another sense, this safety has made us weak. It made us not truly consider the prospect of death, because for most of us, the odds of us suddenly dying on any given day are pretty darn slim. And we as humans actually were not meant to live under such safe circumstances. The way we were meant to live was with the very real prospect that we could die any day, so we always had to be alert, we always had to be ready to fight, we always had to be ready to part with our friends and family (our tribe), because every time we saw them could be our last time with them. And so, back in the day when you saw a woman you wanted to approach, that chance might never ever come again in your life because you might not live to see tomorrow, not to mention the fact that there were just less humans in the world, and so we didn't have the billions of options that we have with women today. And so when you saw a woman, you had to take it seriously because not approaching her would maybe have been messing up the one chance in your life that you had to reproduce, so you really had to approach back then, because another chance to make an approach wouldn't come so easily.

So the question is, how can we instill the fear of death in you (a sense of urgency) when modern life has kind of pushed death way out of most people's minds on a daily basis, when in the past it was something on most people's minds daily? And the answer is that because we do live in such a cozy and friendly society these days, for the most part, we need to make an effort to consciously realize that we are all going to get old and die at some point and that our life on this Earth is short.

Any day alive is a great day, because these great days won't always be there, so we need to be thankful for each and every day that we are alive, because each day is special and truly full of wonder, and if we see a woman that we could approach, even if we live to be over one hundred years old, do we really want to die knowing that we never approached that woman on that one day far in the past, the woman who could have been our future wife. No, we don't want that, we want to have no regrets. In my life, I've had the opportunity to talk to a lot of older men at retirement age, and based on what they've told me, regrets really get to you when you don't have much time left on this Earth. When you get to retirement age, memories become really important, so your memories of having the courage to make an approach, even if you failed it as opposed to never having made the approach will hit you quite differently when you're an old man with not much time left. And the memories we make really do change the type of person we become, because your whole life up to this point has been nothing but a collection of memories, and those memories make you who you are, they really do.

Furthermore, you only have one shot at this life in this world, and so you want to take advantage of it in every way possible and be the best man that you could possibly be, and part of being the best man in the short time you have to live on this Earth is making that approach when the opportunity arises.

If you're the kind of guy who has sat down at a cafe, or pub, or walked around a mall and saw all kinds of beautiful women walking around and you didn't bother to talk to any of them, then what the heck are you even living for, seriously? Like you get one shot at this life, and you're going to let all those opportunities pass you by? You're going to let the years slip by until you're too old to make approaches? Until you've hit retirement age and you're waiting for death? Seriously? Is that what you really want your life to be? A botched-up life full of regrets and failures, because you were too scared to talk to a woman?

Look, there are no do-overs, time will pass faster and faster as you age, so you need to realize that every chance you have to talk to a woman, you'd better take that chance. Yes, you may have a little anxiety before the approach, but you'll feel much better after the approach, because you won't have any regrets. Even if she rejects you, there is nothing to regret there, because you made your approach and gave it your best effort. And taking action when we must, and never having regrets, is what being a man is all about.

So just realize, that although life is pretty safe, you will get old soon, and you will eventually die. Your time is limited on this Earth, so you'd better seize the day and approach the next woman you meet and just say, "Hi, that's a cool-looking shirt," at the very least. Because I'm not making any of this stuff up, and so if you don't focus on making those approaches, years will pass without you making any approaches, and you might find yourself old, still single, and perhaps with no kids, and near death, and how would you like that future? I'm guessing you probably wouldn't like it very much.

So please do keep it top-of-mind, that life is short, that death is coming for you one day, and that you have to make the most of today and make the best memories you possibly can, because you won't have these moments forever, and what could be better than spending these present moments that you do have approaching and talking to a woman that you find attractive, and finding out what she's all about?

That's what life is all about is meeting a woman, it's key for your happiness, for your enjoyment, for you to reproduce, because you'll be dead before you know it, so you need to get on things now, and realize that every chance you have to make an approach that you throw away is truly a wasted opportunity, it really is.

If you feel miserable, well maybe you'll feel better after making an approach. I'll tell you, if I approach a woman and if I get rejected, even if our conversation only went a few seconds, I really do enjoy those few seconds, even getting rejected. So don't be afraid of rejection, enjoy those rejections. When you're an old man, you'll have fond memories of those rejections, trust me.

And I think you get it, that death will get us at one point, so you need to enjoy the now, which is why you really can't afford to waste any time dilly-dallying and not making approaches. You need to approach son, and you need to approach today with a sense of urgency, and do it with a smile on your face and excitement in your eyes, because it is exciting, and it is the very thing that makes life worth living, don't mess up your life for one more day not approaching and not trying to talk to beautiful women, because death is truly nearer than you think. Yes getting to the age of over a hundred may seem very far away, but as previously mentioned, time moves faster and faster as you age, and at an exponential rate, and so it's far closer than you think.

If you needed a wake-up call I hope this is it, wake up! Realize how short your life actually is, and don't waste another second of it!

ONE MORE THING

Beware of procrastination, or telling yourself that you'll do this another day another time, because the more you procrastinate on this the more you'll forget and the less likely the chance you'll do this. When we procrastinate, hours become days, days become weeks, and weeks become years very quickly. You need to start talking to women today, and every day thereafter if possible, and you need to do it with a sense of urgency. Any procrastination on your part is just a way of supplicating to your approach anxiety by telling yourself excuses of why you have to wait 'til yet another day before you can try this stuff out.

I warn you now, don't fall into the procrastination trap, as there is no better time to meet a new woman than the present.

If you're reading this and it's nighttime and you're in bed and want to pass out, I get it. But if it's any other time of day, you don't really have an excuse.

If you're in an area with no women around or you have to be at work, I get it. But you need to make a plan to get yourself to some crowded place where there are a lot of women around, and you need to do it pronto, so that you can start meeting new women today, or at least tomorrow at the very latest.

CHAPTER 16
SEE APPROACH ANXIETY FOR WHAT IT REALLY IS

IF THE LAST two things I mentioned weren't enough to kill your approach anxiety, then I'm hoping what you learn in this chapter will kill your approach anxiety once and for all.

You've noticed that more than once off the first approach of the day I was able to do better with a woman than on following approaches. I thought this was a coincidence at first, but after talking to many other men I realized it wasn't only me. Still though, I chalked this up to coincidence or luck, because there'd be many a time that I'd blow out on the first approach of the day, and do far better on later approaches.

Though it was still odd to me that success off the first approach would continue to happen enough times, that I thought there had to be more to this phenomenon than mere coincidence or luck. And so, I started to begin paying attention to why this would happen, and what I realized was that upon making my first approach of the day, I was always the most nervous, though the moment I said my opener to a woman and she responded, my body would naturally calibrate to show relaxed body language, even though on the inside I'd be freaking out. As I would speak, my mind would be telling me, "don't show your nervousness, appear to be relaxed," and I would listen to that voice. And I realized that what I thought was anxiety or approach anxiety was actually not that at all. Rather it was a fight or flight response. It was adrenaline masked as anxiety. Just this realization alone helped me to make more seemingly natural first approaches of the day.

I'm sure you've heard of humans achieving amazing feets at times when adrenaline courses through their blood, and the first approach of the day is no different. It is, in fact, the first approach that I believe to be the most special approach of the day, because it packs the largest punch of adrenaline. Before your first approach, it feels not so different than sky diving, like you're about to jump out of a plane, but once you jump it starts to be quite enjoyable, and once you land or the interaction is over, you hunger for more and want to skydive again or do another approach.

And so, you need to see approach anxiety for what it really is, adrenaline. This begs the question, why would our body produce adrenaline when we approach a woman we like? And the answer is: Because our body wants us to be successful on that approach, so it's giving us the resources we need in order to be successful. Yes, it's perhaps concerned that another man could kill us or that this may be our one chance in a lifetime at finding that perfect partner for us. But whatever the reason, the fact of the matter is that our body sees our success at the approach as being more important than ever, and so our body is helping us by producing exactly what we need it to produce to be successful.

The first time you ever go skydiving, it will be scary as fuck to jump out of that plane. But you know there are people who do it as a hobby, and then there are army paratroopers who routinely jump out of planes every day as if it were nothing. And approaching women is no different. In fact, the whole point of focusing on approaches is because we want our approaches to go as smoothly as how smooth it looks when we see an army paratrooper jump out of a plane, and it will. I mean, you'll still feel that adrenaline every time, but you can learn to enjoy those jolts of adrenaline and use that adrenaline to help you make your first approach of the day into a better one.

All you really need to do is be aware of what I've said here, right before making your first approach of the day. Meaning that rather than seeing that anxiety you're feeling as approach anxiety, see it for what it really is, which is not approach anxiety at all, but rather Approach Adrenaline. Just the very act of making a mental shift to start seeing approach anxiety as approach adrenaline has done absolute wonders for what used to be a fear for me. Because I now approach women knowing that my body is on my team supporting my efforts by providing me with the perfect cocktail of biological hormones that will give me the best possible chance of making a successful approach.

And now that I've made you aware of it, how could you not forget it? Seriously, just every time prior to that first approach of the day, see your anxiety as an adrenaline helper that your body is producing for you to help you succeed. If you do just that, you'll be making the jump from guy with approach anxiety to army paratrooper pickup artist in no time at all.

CHAPTER 17
THE REST OF THE CONVERSATION WITH JOHN

I INCLUDED this part just in case you wondered how the rest of the conversation went with John. Here it is:

"I promise," I said.

"It's just approaching," John said.

"What?"

"There are no secrets, it's just approaching."

"What do you mean?"

"I mean, all the other secrets that bootcamp instructors claim to help you get women, well there's some truth to them, but there is no real foolproof rule that works across the board, because women are human beings and all human beings are different. The only, one, foolproof thing that absolutely works across the board is approaching and talking to women. I mean if you just have the courage to approach and talk to women, everything else is already built inside of you and will come out naturally."

"No, but that can't be, what about you telling me to compliment clothing, surely that's a technique that most guys don't know, isn't it?" I asked in disbelief of what John was telling me.

"That's just common sense, I mean if you approach a woman, what else are you going to say to her? I mean, you need a topic of conversation, and complimenting her eyes, well that's something she was born with so she's not likely to value that kind of compliment. Complimenting her clothing, on the other hand, is complimenting something she chose, so it's, in essence, indirectly complimenting the effort she put into choosing something, whereas she didn't put any effort into choosing her eyes. You see, a piece of clothing any person chooses is a direct reflection of their personality that we can see, giving us an idea of what their personality is like before actually speaking to them."

"Hmmm, I'd never thought of it like that."

"I get that you'd never thought of it like that, but really that's just common sense."

"But it's common sense I didn't already know, and so it's a secret tactic, no?"

"If you just approach more women, you'd figure that out automatically, because it would be clear that complimenting a woman's natural physical characteristics won't get you as far as complimenting a piece of clothing."

"Hmmm, so you're saying that by just approaching, I'd be able to figure out most things on my own by seeing what gets me further with a woman."

"Exactly, approaching is The Big Secret, everything else is just common sense."

"Are you sure about this?"

"You don't have to believe it, but I'm telling you that's all it is, approaching is everything as far as having lots of options with women, everything else is just fluff."

"Well, what about Abundance Mentality?"

"That's another thing that would come automatically, it's just a common-sense thing that you'd be able to pick up on automatically by just making more approaches. I thought you'd do better to be aware of it early on, since it would help you get the concept quicker, because it took me a lot of time and many approaches to be able to figure that one out. I mean, that's what you're paying for, the knowledge that will help you get better in as short as a time span as possible."

"I see, so you're saying that all I have to do is get good at making approaches and everything else will simply figure itself out."

"Yes."

"So, I didn't even need a bootcamp, I just needed someone to tell me I should be approaching and talking to as many women as possible."

"Yeah, but don't tell anyone else."

"Well, why did you tell me this? I feel like I wasted four thousand on this bootcamp now that I understand there never were any secrets or magic, it was just you telling me to approach different women."

"If I didn't tell you, you would never have known. This is The Big Secret that men who are ultra-successful with women have kept from other men for tens of thousands of years."

"Wait, what? What do you mean for tens of thousands of years?"

"So men figured out early on in our history that approaching was the key to success with women. The men who knew this didn't want other men to know, and kept this secret hidden, and they still keep it hidden today, which is why most of the media and movies you see never get into this fact. In fact, most of the stuff that media and movies tell you will work would actually have the opposite effect in real life. It's because it's still very much hidden."

"What?"

"It's true. And it's hidden for a reason, because the elites who are in the know don't want the common man figuring it out."

"That's pretty mindblowing, I had no idea."

"And now that you know, don't tell anyone."

"Okay, I won't tell anyone."

"It's not me you have to worry about if you tell someone, I mean I broke the rule too, since I told you. But even if you told others, it's not like anyone would believe you. You see society is set up in a way where no one would even believe it if you told them the truth, because the elites don't want others to know. So don't get me wrong, it certainly doesn't bother me who you tell, but it will bother the elites."

"As in, they would kill me if I told?"

"Aha ha, no they probably won't kill you. They probably wouldn't even notice you."

"Well, what if I wrote a book about this stuff?"

"Look, you do what you want, just don't say I'm the one who told you the truth."

"Okay."

"I'm fucking serious Zeph, don't fuck with me! If you fucking name me and one day you don't wake up because your brains somehow ended up splattered against the walls, don't ask who did it."

"Wait! Wha? Are you fucking serious? You're threatening my life over this?"

"Knowing what you know now, do you still even want the three phone calls?"

"Yes, I do."

"So you still think there is something else that I know and you don't, and that it's not just approaches?"

"I'm not so sure."

"Well, I told you the truth for what it's worth, even if you can't believe it right now, and I'll do my best to give you the right advice should you need to call me."

"Great, thank you so much, Sensei."

"Just don't fucking name me or you're a dead man Zeph, Capeesh?"

"Jesus fucking Christ John, you're scaring the fuck out of me! I swear on my ancestors I will never ever ever ever fucking name you."

"I like the sincerity of your answer, Zeph. Good."

So now you know what was said, and now you know what to do, and you already know how to get over your approach anxiety. So what's going to happen now? Well, I'm not going to tell you anything, because you should already know what to do.

If you don't know what to do then something is wrong and perhaps you should reread all parts of this book up to this point, because you're not getting any younger just sitting there. Times a ticking, and time is something that you really don't have much of.

I don't care what age you are, whether you're in your early twenties or late fifties, time is of the essence, because every day that passes you simply cannot get back.

There is no better day to try out what you've learned in this book than today, because the more time that elapses the harder it's going to be to get yourself to approach and talk to women, because you'll soon forget what you read here and you'll once again be fed information by the media and movies trying to convince you that approaching women isn't the way to meet women.

CHAPTER 18
NATURALS

AFTER MY LAST conversation with John, and before I got engaged, I did massive amounts of approaches daily for a good long while. And during that time I began to notice that I wasn't the only one approaching women, because I'd be looking around for a woman to approach, and I'd see another guy just go up and make an approach.

At first, I thought these other men must have also taken John's bootcamp, but I wasn't sure, so I decided to approach each man I saw making approaches after they parted ways with whatever woman they were talking to, and I was surprised at what I had found.

And what I found was that only a minority of the men I saw doing approaches considered themselves pickup artists, and pickup artists who didn't take a bootcamp with John, but rather pickup artists who had taken a bootcamp with one of John's competitors.

Though the funny part was that the vast majority of men I saw doing approaches didn't consider themselves to be pickup artists at all, rather they were what the pickup artist community calls naturals.

There was one natural in particular called Sam that I was

extremely curious about, because he was a much older man than I, seemed like he was in his fifties but I didn't ask, and I was surprised at how effortlessly he seemed approaching and number-closing women, so I decided to take him out for a steak to ask all about where he had learned to game the way he does.

As it turned out, he didn't really know what game was at all and said he had always just approached and talked to women. "It's just natural, if you see a woman you like you go on up and talk to her," he told me.

This was shocking to me, that he knew the secret of how to meet women for his entire life, no one taught him how to do it, he had no approach anxiety at all, and just talked to women whenever he felt like it.

Sam was the epitome of a natural to me and became a good friend of mine. When I tried to explain to him about how it wasn't at all natural for me, and how hard it was for me to just go up and talk to women, his response to that was, "Yeah, some men just aren't good with women."

I realized during that conversation that I'd never be a natural, but I do fully understand now that there are a good number of naturals out there who are not so different than Sam. The only difference between naturals and guys who learn game is that naturals always knew game, it just came naturally to them from a young age. To them, doing game was not so different than how natural it was for me to drink water, jog, or do anything else that I just naturally know how to do.

I'm not sure why approaching and talking to women came naturally to naturals and not to other men, but I so wished that I could have been a natural.

What I did take away from seeing naturals in action was that there was no point even comparing my game to them, because my game would never be like that of a natural. I'd always have to consciously be aware of what I was doing and push myself to make approaches, very much unlike a natural who would approach and talk to women calmly and confidently without even thinking about it.

Though, I did wonder if I kept making an effort to approach and talk to women long enough, if I could eventually be at the same level of a natural, as in just approaching and talking to women without even thinking about it very much the same way I'd make myself a glass of water and drink it without thinking about it. However, I don't think myself or most guys who learn to approach and talk to women will ever really know the answer to that, because if we keep approaching and talking to women, most of us will at some point want to have a girlfriend and perhaps even get engaged and get married, which means we stop doing game and never find out how far we could have actually progressed had we not settled down and continued year after year to keep making regular approaches.

And I guess it doesn't even matter to find out if we could ever get to the level of a natural or not, because the moment we get what we want out of game, which for most men will be a girlfriend, then there isn't really a point to continue doing approaches unless we get to a point where things with our girlfriend don't work out.

CHAPTER 19
DATING APP TRAP

SOCIETY WILL TELL YOU, why do you need to do all this hard work approaching women? Why not just try a dating app? They'll try to convince you that it's a better way. And why is society trying to convince you to just use dating apps, well it's because society's opinions on the matter have been shaped by the marketing machine of the dating app companies, and those companies want nothing more than for you to think dating apps is the only way to meet women, so that they can profit off your women problems.

Now I'm not going to tell you that dating apps don't work, they definitely can work, but they just don't work as well as approaching a woman face-to-face.

It's very easy to get sucked into dating apps, get addicted to dating apps, and spend a lot of time, hours upon hours, using them, and then getting little to no results. I would actually say, don't use them at all, you'd be much better off not touching them.

However, if you were at some point going to dabble with a dating app, because you wanted to try it out, then I'd say before you go the dating app route, first build up your game through doing real-life face-to-face approaches, and once you get a lot better at approaching and talking to women, it's then okay to use dating apps as a supplement to a regular approach routine, but don't ever rely on dating apps as a substitute for approaching and talking to women, because the truth of the matter is that dating apps don't actually work that well as compared to approaching women you see around you in real life.

Also, a lot of women's photos on those apps are often photos they took years ago or are photoshopped in some way, so when you meet them in real life, they often look quite different than what they look like in the dating app. But when you approach a woman in real life, what you see is exactly what you get, unlike a dating app. Actually, that's one of the great parts of approaching women, the fact that you can see what a woman is like in real life before you approach her.

Anyway, I did try dating apps once, and let me tell you, the results I got approaching women face-to-face were of a night and day difference, as in when I'd approach and talk to women I got a ton of results, got into conversations instantly which made me feel less lonely, and always felt better and more confident about myself after having made an approach. But with dating apps, they caused me to feel more and more introverted each time I used them, like they were killing my game as opposed to helping it, and I always felt that I could do better doing approaches than whatever a dating app could do for me.

You see on these apps, women judge you by things like your age and photos, and some women will actually filter men out by age, height, and other things that are completely unrelated to our personality, but with doing approaches, they're judging you mostly based just on your personality and how you present yourself.

Doing approaches has so many advantages over dating apps that I could go on and on forever about it. Yes, dating apps mean you don't have to approach women, but at the same time, it also means you won't build the skills necessary to really understand women like you would by approaching women. And so, you'll more often than not fail with those women you meet on the apps due to not having have developed the skill of being good with women which can only be developed through having the courage to simply approach and talk to women in real life.

Anyway, I'll never touch a dating app again, just a time drain in my opinion. Up to you if you want to try them.

And the takeaway is, if you want to dabble with dating apps, then fine, but only do so after you first build up your game through doing real-life face-to-face approaches. Though probably better to just never touch dating apps in the first place and pretend they don't exist.

CHAPTER 20
COMMON SENSE THINGS TO HELP YOUR GAME

THERE ARE a lot of common sense things that can greatly help your game, and I shouldn't have to mention these things, because they are common sense, but I will mention them because a lot of people (myself included) tend to forget or lose track of what is just plain common sense. So here is a list of common sense things that if you're not doing, you need to be doing:

Eat Right

I'm not a doctor, and if you need medical advice you should seek it, so don't go changing your diet because of what I'm telling you here without consulting with your doc first. But as common sense would dictate, you need to be eating right and getting yourself to a normal healthy weight. Based upon all my experience, this means avoiding anything with added sugar, avoiding any processed foods as much as possible, and avoiding anything high in salts or saturated fats. Rather, you need to be eating whole and unprocessed foods. I'm not a vegan or vegetarian, but even on those diets, the same applies, eat whole and unprocessed foods. This means you eat meat, fish, eggs, vegetables, and fruit is okay too, and if you're a vegetarian you'd cut out the meat and fish, and if you're a vegan you'd cut out the meat, fish, and eggs. And as far as what to drink, you drink only water and avoid processed sugary drinks, like soda, energy drinks, and sugar-loaded coffee drinks. As I said, I'm not a doctor, and I'm not telling you what kind of diet to do, definitely do consult with your doctor, but to me this is just common sense that we get our diet right. Diet is the most foundational thing, because it's where our energy comes from, and it's the key to looking our best, and not just in regards to body shape but also in regards to the vibrance and health that can be seen in our skin and eyes. Yes, I think what we eat does make a difference as to how healthy we look when we're talking to women, and it does make a difference as far as how well our brain functions and how quickly we react when we're talking to women.

Exercise

Another thing that you need to do as a man, is you need to be exercising or weight lifting even. And again, I'm not a doctor and so I'm not going to suggest what kind of workout program you do, and do consult a doctor before making any changes to your exercise routine, but if your BMI is not in the normal range, you need to do something about that. And if you don't even know what a BMI is, then you need to take a closer look at where your health is at and get things in line. As for me, I make sure to walk at least 10,000 steps a day, and you tend to do a lot of walking when you're looking for women to approach and talk to, and I hit the gym 2 to 3 times a week. It's just common sense to me that one would exercise, or at least walk, and try to get their BMI in the normal range if it's not already there. Other people can definitely tell when they look at us how physically fit we look, and while looking physically fit alone won't necessarily get the ladies, it definitely helps. Because when you look good, you feel good, and when you feel good, you're going to naturally walk and talk more confidently, which is going to help increase how attractive you look to women. You don't have to look like a model, and it's fine to have defects whatever they may be, but as long as you're doing things to look as good as you can on a daily basis, it's definitely going to be noticeable, and it sends signals to women that you're a man who's got his priorities in order, which is definitely a turn-on compared to if you're a man who doesn't have his priorities in order.

Sleep

Once again, this is not medical advice, seek a doctor if you need medical advice. But common sense would also dictate that you get enough sleep every night so you don't look like a tired mess. By getting enough sleep, you're going to be more alert, and you'll do better when you're having conversations with women. There is no bigger turn-off to a woman than a guy who is visibly falling asleep as she's talking to him.

Grooming Habits

You don't have to be the best at grooming yourself, but you should be showering, and if you smell you should be using soap at the very least. The better your grooming habits, the more likely you are to be accepted by not just other women, but also other people in general. Because no one likes talking to a person who smells or has bad breath, etc, so you need to be aware of how well-groomed you are.

Fashion

Women don't expect men to know anything about fashion, and a lot of men look great in just jeans and a T-shirt. But if you're totally clueless about fashion, it doesn't hurt to take up an interest in fashion and at least show you're making an effort to be fashionable, which basically means wearing clothing that generally looks good on you. And if you're truly clueless about this, you might want to ask someone you know who's into fashion how you could change your look. But even if you don't know anyone into fashion, all you have to do is find your local mall, enter a few clothing stores that carry clothing for men, and spend a little time talking to the staff and tell them you're trying to look more fashionable and ask them what they recommend. Fashion isn't everything, but it definitely can make a man look more interesting. And if you don't have the perfect body shape yet, choosing the right kind of fashion can definitely change that for you and make you look a whole lot cooler.

All these things I just mentioned are each just a small part of what can make you more attractive to a woman, but if you give a little attention to each of them, it all adds up to giving you just a little bit of an edge over if you didn't do all these things, and every little edge you can get will definitely help your game, trust me on that.

CHAPTER 21
TWO MINDSET IMPLEMENTATIONS

THIS IS NOT A SECRET, and you already know The Big Secret, which is that approaching is what it's all about. Rather this is about things that are perhaps not so common sense that will greatly aid you in being a better man, a man that anyone would enjoy talking to. And if you simply try to implement the 2 things we discuss below into your mindset, it's sure to help you.

#1. Don't Be a Complainer

There are many men who like to complain about this, that, and about everything else as their regular mode of conversation. If you're one of those kinds of men, you need to catch yourself when you start to complain and not do it. Being a complainer is the furthest thing from an attractive personality that there is, no one likes a complainer and that includes women, and you need to not be one.

Best to never complain about anything. The only exception is if, for example, you order something in a restaurant and the waiter gets your order wrong, it's okay to complain about something like that, but your complaint should be directed at the waiter or at the restaurant and once the issue is resolved you should stop talking about it. However, what you should definitely not do is be someone who complains about everything just for the sake of complaining.

#2. Be Non-judgmental

What does it mean to be non-judgmental? It means exactly what it says, to not judge people, as in to not think or say that someone is this or that type of person without even knowing the full story of the person you're judging. Like maybe a store clerk doesn't say "Have a good day" to you, and if you judge that they're a rude person off of that one interaction, you might be missing the fact that perhaps their grandma died that morning so they're not in the best of moods today. People have bad days, and just because they don't act ideally doesn't give you the right to judge them based on just one interaction, and if you do so then you'd be a judgmental person.

If a woman gets a sense that you are trying to judge her based on things she does or says, more often than not she won't like that and she won't be hanging around you very long. This doesn't just apply if you're judging the woman but also applies to if you're judging anyone. Like, let's say you're at a cafe with a woman and you make some judgmental comments about another person at the cafe. The comment doesn't have to be to that person's face, but it could be whispered to your date. Well, what that judgmental comment says about you is that you are a judgmental person which means that even though you're judging someone else and not your date that you will likely judge your date at one point in the future, and this is a turn-off, and even if a woman doesn't tell you this to your face, she's thinking it. The judgmental comment could be as simple as saying, "That barista is a little weird," and that's enough to lose the respect of the woman you're with and cause her to never want to see you again.

If you were never a complainer or never judgmental, then you don't have to worry about these things at all, but if you do tend to complain and do tend to be on the judgmental side, then you're best to not vocalize those thoughts and instead smile at the woman you're with and talk about something else.

CHAPTER 22
COMMON PITFALLS

OKAY, this book wouldn't be complete if we didn't get into some common pitfalls:

A Woman's Tests

Sometimes when talking to women who already seem interested and receptive to you, she might suddenly throw out some negative comments, essentially insulting you. What she's usually doing here is basically giving you a test, checking to see if you're going to get upset, or if you're going to remain unphased. If you get upset, you fail her test, her attraction for you drops and the conversation could be over.

The whole key when a woman says something negative is to be unphased by it. You could just stare into her eyes, half smiling, and say something like, "Are you serious?" and then laugh. If she also laughs then you passed her test. Another thing you could do is you could bring up some other topic like you didn't even notice what she just said, and if she then changes and starts talking about the other topic with you, then you pass the test. A third thing you could do is just look at her and laugh, as if you saw her sudden negative comment as a joke. All of these things work because they show you're unphased. However, if you take what she says seriously and you get upset, you won't pass her test.

I myself failed these tests at first not realizing why it happened, but after learning that remaining unphased is the key to passing these tests, I was able to easily pass all of them. And every time you pass these tests, the woman will become more attracted to you. A woman only tests you because she's attracted to you in the first place, and because she's hoping you'll pass her test so she can become more attracted to you. You should also note that a woman will keep testing you every now and then throughout your relationship with her, and the way to pass those tests is always the same, remain unphased.

One note on this point, and that is that you should not confuse rejection for tests. If a woman insults you in some way it's a test, but if a woman makes it clear that your presence is not welcome, then you'd better get out of there right away before she dumps her drink in your face and then follows that up by throwing nuts in your face.

Texting

A lot of guys who get a woman's number might find that she will start texting. The main thing with texting is to not get into chit-chatting with her through text, and use texting only for scheduling to see her. If she texts you something about her day, it's polite to text something back when you have time to, but don't get into a big conversation through text. Also, I would recommend not to text her back the moment you receive a text from her, because it shows that you have nothing better to do than wait for her texts which will drop her attraction for you, better to text back later.

Dating

A lot of guys think going on a date with a woman is different than the approach, but really it's not. Dating is just a way to continue where you left off from when you last talked to her. There is no need to try to impress a woman when going out on a date with her, so don't try to impress her, because she'll see any attempt to impress her as a needy move. The best rule when going out on a date with a woman is to do something casual with her that you want to do or need to do anyway.

When or How to Get Her Into Bed

A lot of guys feel unsure of when or how to get her into bed, and so did I. Honestly speaking, and I know you're sick of hearing me say this, but it's another common sense thing. What I mean is, if you get along with her, and she gets along with you, and she seems attracted to you which you can tell by the fact that she keeps coming out to meet you and keeps giving you googly eyes, then it's likely that she's considered the possibility that if you two were alone in a room together that things might start to get a whole lot more interesting.

Anyway, what you do is you simply put it out there that you'd like to invite her to your place to hang out further. If she excitedly accepts your offer to go to your place to hang out further, that's a good sign, you're going to your place with a woman, yeah! Don't get too excited though, maintain your composure.

Once you get to your place you simply hang out with her there, eat, talk, show her something about your place, and then you can ask her if she wants to hang out in your bedroom. If she excitedly accepts your offer to hang out in your bedroom, well then it's likely going to be a good night for you. If you're stuck as to how to move forward in the bedroom, then you can ask her to teach you what to do if you need to. If she's excitedly entered your bedroom it likely means she's really attracted to you, so she should be definitely glad to be the lucky one to show you the ropes. Also, be sure to ask for consent before doing each activity you want to do, and she should also be asking you for consent as well for each activity she wants to do. Also, please be aware of your local laws as far as what consent is and what consent is not and all that, and please be sure to abide by them.

CHAPTER 23
RELATIONSHIPS

THE WORD "RELATIONSHIP" is a very loosely defined term, it can mean many things, but generally in life (depending on what culture you come from) there will be three categories that relationships fall into, and those categories are: Friends, Family, and Partner. And it should be obvious due to the nature of this book that the only category of relationship that we're going to talk about will be the relationship with a partner.

A relationship with a partner can start the first minute you talk to a woman, because that first minute can easily turn into decades before you know it. Though generally, a relationship with a partner will be somewhere on a spectrum of: 1. I Just Met This Woman, 2. We're Dating, 3. She's My Girlfriend, 4. We're Engaged, 5. She's My Wife.

Most of the women you approach will fall into the I Just Met This Woman part of the spectrum, but that could easily turn into We're Dating, sometimes on the same day even, and you can find yourself to be still in the We're Dating part of the spectrum months down the line, or even years down the line in some cases.

Anyway, if you like a woman and if she likes you as well,

and if you want to get into a relationship with her, that's your prerogative, and you can feel free to do so. If getting into a relationship is what you really want, then as long as you and your partner have communicated about it and you're both on the same page, and both want the same things, then all should be good.

I would just say if at any point you're having some doubts about the relationship, the sooner you end it the better. Because the longer you stick in a relationship you're doubting, the harder you'll find it to get out of that relationship.

If you meet a woman you like and she also likes you, you're likely to enter the We're Dating part of the spectrum very soon. However, as a man, you need to be heavily filtering women before you go too deep down the We're Dating path. Filtering women means you need to be on the lookout for lies, deceit, trickery, and any number of traits that would mean the woman wouldn't make a good long-term partner. Though do not confuse a woman's tests as being a red flag, because all a woman's tests are is her checking you to make sure that you don't have any red flags about you as well.

If there are no red flags you find about a woman, that doesn't mean some won't surface later. I've heard stories from other men where red flags surfaced years later. And anyway, the burden is on you to decide how far you'd like to take your relationship with a woman. In my case, I've decided to get engaged and get married, but it doesn't mean you have to follow in my footsteps. You should do whatever you feel comfortable with, and don't let anyone pressure you into something that you don't feel comfortable with.

The thing about a relationship with a partner is that no one can really advise you on it, and it's really up to you and your partner as to how far you want to take things. I do have a word of advice for you though, and that is that if a woman ever does something that disturbs you deeply and doesn't apologize for it, then it's in your best interest to end the relationship no matter how much you like her. And the reason is that if she did something messed up once, she's likely to do it again, and it will be worse the second time, and even worse the third time.

And this brings us to the next thing we need to go over, and that is Toxic Relationships. If you find yourself in a position when you're with a woman who you really like on a physical level, but on a mental level it seems like it's more pain than it's worth, you know you're going to need to reject this woman. Because continuing on in a relationship that you find to be stressful is what many would call a toxic relationship, and the deeper you get into one of those kinds of relationships the harder it's going to be to get out.

Basically, if a woman causes you any kind of major stress that causes you to feel really bad, then it means the relationship has become toxic and it's time to get out, because the longer you stay in a relationship like that the worst you'll feel. So it's good to get out of that kind of relationship as soon as possible.

A toxic relationship usually seems good at first, that's why people get into them, but the toxicity develops slowly, and some men don't realize it or even know what they're dealing with until it's too late or until they get married and their life gets turned upside down by it.

You don't want to be one of those men who gets destroyed by entering into a toxic relationship. Therefore, you need to look for the red flags so that it doesn't happen to you. However, there are so many different red flags to look for depending on what you're dealing with that it can be hard to spot for the average man who is not pursuing a university degree in psychology.

Though there's no need to worry because there's one telltale sign, and that sign is exactly what I stated, if one thing happens that makes you feel really bad, and especially if the woman doesn't recognize how bad you feel or make any effort to apologize, then you can be sure it's time to get out.

If it's early in the relationship, then getting out is easy and is best done by text. All you do is prepare a farewell text, which should basically state that you can never see her or talk to her again, and that's it. Don't get into what she did that caused you to end the relationship and don't get into the things you don't like about her. And what you do next is send the text, and then block her everywhere and anywhere where she may try to contact you. If you've been seeing this woman for a month or more, it may be really hard to do that, but you need to do that. Because if you don't do that things can get far worse, and you don't want to be there when they do get far worse. Hopefully, such a relationship hasn't gone a month or more and you were able to notice something is not right early on.

If the relationship has gone on for many months or even years or you're married to the woman, then it's going to be a bit more complicated on how you end things, and I can't even give you advice on that, you may even need a lawyer in that case.

The point I'm making is that It's always better to end things sooner than later when it comes to these things, because the longer you wait the harder it will be and the worse things will get. So if something that hurts you happens in the relationship and you think you'll just let it slide or ignore it, think again, because that's a sign telling you to end things.

How bad can it get? You don't even want to know, and you want to end it before you find out.

CHAPTER 24
COMING TO A CLOSE

NOW THIS BOOK is coming to a close, and I hope that you've come away with something, and that something I've stated here will aid you in your life.

If nothing else I've said meant anything to you, you should at least understand that the whole secret to game is just one thing and only one thing, and that is that you need to practice approaching and talking to women, because really that's all there is to game or pickup artistry, there is nothing else (and even outside of pickup artistry, it's exactly what naturals do).

If you just focus on using whatever works for you to get over your approach anxiety, and focus on getting better at approaching and talking to women, then everything else will automatically fall into place for you.

There is nothing more I can tell you or teach you other than: Approach! Approach! Approach!

And if you come to me with a question on anything about game or women, my answer to you would be only one word, and that word would be: Approach!

Seriously, there is nothing to teach in regards to game, because once you know that all you have to do is Approach women, you're going to figure out everything else on your own, and you will naturally adapt to whatever obstacles women throw your way. This is the beauty of nature, that as male specimens of the human species, we have an innate ability to adapt to whatever life throws our way, and this includes encounters with the opposite sex.

Therefore, if you understand the one lesson that this book has taught you, which is to approach, and if you actually do it, meaning you actually make an effort to approach and talk to women, then your body, your mind, and even your DNA will all adapt to those circumstances and you'll keep getting better at it the more you do it.

There is nothing more for you to learn here, and now that you know it, if you were to put down this book right now, you'd know what you need to do. The reason all the other dating gurus and courses don't tell you that all you really need to do is to stop learning about game and just focus on approaching and talking to women is simply because they'd have nothing to sell you if they convinced you that that's all there was to it, and, surprise-surprise, that's really all there is to it.

And so if you got nothing else out of this book, but understood the main message that I've been trying to hammer into your head, which is: Approach! Then you are all set, and if you actually make an effort to take action and start making approaches, then any of the women problems you've ever had will melt away, because you'll soon have so many options with women that you won't even understand how it was that you used to have women problems.

So please take what I'm saying to heart, and just do the obvious, Approach! And keep approaching! And make it a consistent part of your regular routine, just like making time to eat breakfast or anything else. Make some time every day, or every week, to get your approaches in, and keep at it consistently. Consistency is key here, like anything else that you want to improve in. Want to have big muscles? Then you'd better be lifting weights on a regular schedule consistently. Want to get good with women? Then you'd better be approaching and talking to women consistently. It really is that simple.

CHAPTER 25
OBJECTIONS

OF COURSE, some of you are going to have some objections to everything that I've said. The common objections many men will have are:

I Don't Look Good Enough

Although I happened to be tall, I never considered myself to be a good-looking man. I'm not going to say that looks don't matter at all, but they are certainly not everything. No matter how you look, if you try your best to take care of yourself, and if you try your best to keep approaching and talking to women, what you'll find is that some women will still be into you regardless of you not looking like a model.

The fact is that no matter what you look like, you have a unique personality, and you bring a unique perspective to the world, and while every woman will not be into you, some definitely will, so it's very much a numbers game of finding those women who will overlook your looks and will like you based on your personality. And there is no better way to put the odds of that numbers game in your favor than by continuing to make a consistent effort to regularly approach and talk to women.

However, if you are a man who is truly fixated on the fact that you think you don't look good enough, then you may also need to talk to a medical professional on what you can do about it. There are many things men can do to improve their looks, from choosing the right clothes, to working out, to eating a better diet, all of which we've already talked about in this book. However, if none of those will work for you, then seeing a medical professional to help you get whatever the problem is handled will likely be the best way to go.

I'm Not Rich Enough

Money isn't everything, but it is true that some women only go for rich men. Though you don't have to be rich, because the vast majority of women aren't attracted to only rich men. So regardless of what's in your bank account, if you keep approaching and talking to women, you're sure to find a woman who won't care about how much money you have. So not being rich enough is a non-issue when it comes to these things. There is definitely a reason the phrase "money can't buy love" has become so popular, and that's because it really can't. While money can buy you a heck of a lot, you can't buy your way into a woman's heart. Sure, some women will take your money if you try to buy her heart, but there won't be any kind of lasting or genuine attraction there.

That's Not Going to Work Attitude

There is always some guy who has what I like to call a "That's Not Going to Work Attitude," who thinks that regard-less of everything I've said that approaching and talking to women will simply not work for them because they just suck with women.

And what I have to say to you is, I used to suck with women, I used to be just like you, but I decided to change my way of thinking, and accept that I was perhaps wrong for all the years that I wasted doing nothing, and not even knowing that approaching and talking to women was an option. I know it's hard to admit it when we're wrong about something, but you can't possibly know that what I'm proposing, approaching and talking to women, won't work for you if you haven't even tried it. If you just want to be a Negative Nellie and assume you're right and that it won't work for you without giving it a go, without even trying, then neither I nor anyone else is going to ever change your mind about that and nothing will ever change for you.

However, if you're willing to accept that what you've been doing so far hasn't been working for you, and if you're willing to humor me and at least try what I'm proposing that you do, then you may just find that you can meet new women, get better at talking to women, and eventually get yourself into a relationship with the right woman. But you need to, first of all, change your attitude and accept that you don't know everything, and that perhaps working on getting better at approaching and talking to women was all you ever needed to do in order to get good with women. It's kind of your call, but if you feel what I'm saying truly won't work for you, then do whatever you want, because I don't think I'm going to change your mind if you're going to be stubborn and so sure that something won't work for you.

If it's not one of those three issues, and if the issue is not approach anxiety (which we've already covered), then I can't imagine any other issue that you could have, other than perhaps a medical issue of another sort. And if it is a medical issue of another sort, then you need to be consulting with a doctor on what to do about it. But pretty much, for most men, the only objections I can see would be one of the three mentioned above, all of which I've addressed.

CHAPTER 26
EMAIL LIST

MY PUBLISHER, Soy Sauce Publishing, runs a secret newsletter called Real Game, where you can get notifications about new books similar to this one, as well as various discounts and special offers.

Also, I may sometimes write to you through this newsletter, so if you want to hear more from me, subscribing to Real Game is the best way to do that.

To join Real Game, all you need to do is go to the following URL:

SoySaucePublishing.com/RealGame

CHAPTER 27
SO NOW WHAT?

OH, and you're still here?

Well, if you're still here, you're probably wondering what you should do now. Well, if you've read this book and didn't just skip to the last chapter, then I think you can probably answer that question yourself because you should already know what I'm going to say.

Just in case you didn't know though, I'm going to tell you to put this book down and get on out there and start approaching and talking to women today, or as soon as is possible, while this is all fresh in your mind.

As we already know, most men won't approach and talk to women, and that is exactly the reason why most men either take the first woman who's into them or simply give up on women altogether, because they don't realize that it's their job to be the one to approach a woman and initiate a conversation with her. You should not be one of those men who doesn't approach women, I was one of those men for most of my life, and I'm telling you my life is a lot better now that I've figured out how to approach women and know what to do.

And now it's up to you to figure out the same things I did, and the best way to do that is to push yourself to approach women. Yes, it's hard, and yes every voice in your head will come up with a reason to not approach women. It seems so easy to just put it off and say to yourself, "I'll start next week," and then next week you might find yourself saying to yourself, "I'll start next month." And if you get into that habit, literally your whole life will pass you by and you'll be old before you know it.

If you really understood all the things I've told you in this book, then you know that not approaching is not an option, and you're going to need to dig deep inside of yourself and find that courage to go out, find women, and approach them. And yes, there is literally no better time than today to start doing that.

Most people fail with women, because they never even have the courage to make their first approach, but trust me, it does get easier, you just have to try making a first one. You'll get better on the next one, and get even better on the one after that.

If what I wrote in this book made any sense to you at all, then I think you understand the situation here, and I think you also understand that your dating life is very much in your own hands.

And so, I highly urge you not to procrastinate, and use what you've learned in this book to jump in the deep end of the pool and get yourself wet. Because you'll be a better and much happier man if you make an approach today and keep up the habit of making regular approaches for many months or years to come. You'd be surprised at how your life changes in so many good ways just by making approaching and talking to women a part of your daily life. It's up to you though, because it is your life.

All that I know is if I had read a book like this years back, I would have taken it seriously and started taking action back then. My biggest regret in life was not knowing what I've told you, and missing out on all those years where I could have been meeting new women.

Yes, your mind perhaps is already trying to work against you, trying to engineer a reason why you can't just go out and meet and talk with women. And I say that whatever reason your mind is telling you, you need to ignore it, because the truth of the matter is that men who do well with women approach and talk to women regularly and you need to start somewhere, and there is no better starting point than making your first approach today.

If you feel nervous, I get it, I was there. And I'm telling you to go somewhere in your area where you know many women will be, and just walk up to one and compliment her shirt, and should she reject you, then walk up to another and compliment her hat, and then approach just one more after that. And if all three reject you, then you need to think about why you were rejected, perhaps the woman you approached already had a boyfriend, or perhaps something about your approach could have been improved. After you think about it, then try yet again, and then again, and don't stop trying. Each rejection isn't neces-sarily a bad thing, because with each rejection you learn some-thing, which will make all of your future approaches better. Rejection is normal, and part of the process, and you need to expect a lot of rejections before things start to make more sense.

But if you hadn't even made one approach yet, then you haven't even taken the first step towards the start of your journey, and that's fine if you simply want to get old and never have any women in your life. The choice is yours. But what I'm saying is you need to make your first approach as soon as is humanly possible, and if that one doesn't work so well, then you need to follow that up with some more approaches! Take what you will from that.

Anyway, I hope you've already put this book down and decided to take my advice and do the right thing.

I just know you're going to get good at this stuff if you keep at it, so hope you'll keep going and not give up at the first sign of rejection. Rejection is simply the universe's way of telling you that you're on the right path. I mean, just think of anyone who got good at anything, they all faced rejection and sucked at first. Essentially, you have to see rejections as a challenge and use them as fuel to keep making approaches.

Wait, why are you still here? Are you still reading? What are you doing? Why aren't you out there talking to women? You are single, right? Then get up off your rump, and get out there right now and start talking to women! And do it now! Sheesh!

Best of luck to you out there in the field!